CREATE CAPTIVATING CLASSES

Why NCLB Should Mean No Child Left Bored

Christopher Bontjes

ROWMAN & LITTLEFIELD EDUCATION
A division of
ROWMAN & LITTLEFIELD PUBLISHERS, INC.
Lanham • New York • Toronto • Plymouth, UK

Published by Rowman & Littlefield Education
A division of Rowman & Littlefield Publishers, Inc.
A wholly owned subsidiary of The Rowman & Littlefield Publishing Group, Inc.
4501 Forbes Boulevard, Suite 200, Lanham, Maryland 20706
www.rowman.com

10 Thornbury Road, Plymouth PL6 7PP, United Kingdom

Copyright © 2013 by Christopher Bontjes

All rights reserved. No part of this book may be reproduced in any form or by any electronic or mechanical means, including information storage and retrieval systems, without written permission from the publisher, except by a reviewer who may quote passages in a review.

British Library Cataloguing in Publication Information Available

Library of Congress Cataloging-in-Publication Data

ISBN 978-1-61048-970-6 (cloth)—ISBN 978-1-61048-971-3 (pbk.)—ISBN 978-1-61048-972-0 (electronic)

To Julie:
My wife, my partner,
my best friend,
and my best audience.

CONTENTS

Foreword by Stephen G. Peters	ix
Preface	xi
Who Is This Guy?	xi
The Big Idea: My "Aha" Moments	xii
Introduction	xv

PART I ENTERTAINING

1 Attention, Please! — 3
    Your Competition — 6
    Work versus Fun? Motivation to Learn — 7
    Entertaining Lessons: Time Wasters or Time Savers? — 8

2 Anatomy of Character — 11
    Creating Your Character — 15
    Mirror, Mirror — 18
    Priority One — 20

3 The Power of Laughter — 23
    Learning to Be Funny — 25
    Funny Is as Funny Does — 27
    Targets for Humor — 29

	The Best Source of Humor	29
	Callbacks and Running Gags	31
	Sight Gags	32
	Ad-libbing: Making It Up as You Go?	34
	Ad-libs and Music	37
	Stepping on a Laugh	37
4	Hecklers	39
	Pacing	41
	Brain Overload	43
5	Creating Interest	45
	But Isn't That ... *Lying*?	49
6	Does This Ring a "Bell?"	51
	Bell Curves and Hecklers	55

PART II PUTTING A SHOW TOGETHER

7	Routine (Lesson) Design	61
	Start at the End	62
8	The Hook	65
9	Getting There Is Half the Fun	69
10	Following the Yellow Brick Road	73
11	If the Shoe Fits ... Teach It	79
	Putting Together a Full Show	81
	How Routine Development Relates to Lesson Plans	82
12	Getting Your Feet Wet	83

PART III SELLING IT

13	How Much Is That Lesson in the Window?	89
14	Your Rapport Card	95
15	Highly Effective Habits	99
	More Information on Sales Techniques	104

PART IV MARKETING

16	Becoming the Pied Piper	107
	Research and Development	109
17	Weapons of Mass Instruction	111
	Reciprocation	111
	Authority	112
	Scarcity	115
	Commitment and Consistency	118
	Liking	120
	Humor	122
18	Liking, Association, and Dog Training	125
	More Information	128

PART V LOOSE ENDS

19	Tying Up Loose Ends	131
	Five and Forty-five	131
20	The (Rail)Roads of Change	135
21	GIGO	139
	The Next Step	140
	A Final Thought	141
	About the Author	143

FOREWORD

Never has there been a better time than now for teachers and school leaders to have a resource like *Create Captivating Classes* at their disposal to offset the unique changes and challenges this new generation of learners brings to us. Unfettered by a prescriptive set of general and specific strategies, this book focuses more on the underlying belief systems that drive behavior. Christopher Bontjes does a masterful job of simplifying the complexity, as he offers helpful tips for every teacher, both new and experienced.

We often wonder, as we read school mission statements that echo the sentiment that "all students can learn," why aren't they then learning? This book provides helpful tips for teachers who may be struggling with the real challenges of reaching today's students and insights for experienced teachers to consider in better understanding these same students. Public education is in dire need of a new system of thought, which requires a new era of thinkers. Bontjes is one of these "new thinkers," who is far beyond thinking "outside the box!" In his book, he has thought his way into the hearts and minds of those of us who struggle daily to answer the call to educate every child we have been so fortunate to meet and teach.

As we continue to be change agents with a renewed sense of purpose and engagement, works like these energize us to begin the classroom transformation process. When we solve the problems for underachieving students, we solve the problems for all students. The factory model, one size fits all, isn't working for anyone. We must ensure all students are academically successful by creating a culture of learning that uses best practices in teaching. The work Christopher Bontjes has created lays a solid foundation for teachers and creates the conditions for effective teaching and learning to take place. As a result, many teachers will experience the joy of capturing and inspiring their students on a daily basis using purpose-driven instruction with incredible results. These carefully thought out and proven strategies will make even the mediocre teacher rise to higher expectations.

Stephen G. Peters, EdS

PREFACE

WHO IS THIS GUY?

I am a teacher.

For more than twenty years I have taught public school students ranging in age from kindergarten through high school. I have also taught adult students via college and community education courses. I have taught in schools in white-collar and blue-collar communities and in affluent and high-poverty areas. I have taught groups ranging in size from private instruction through well over one hundred at a time. I have taught in classrooms, in hallways, and in storage closets.

I am also a magician.

I have been a magician longer—in fact, for my entire life. Both my parents were magicians. I attended my first magicians' convention when I was four months old and performed in my first show at four years old. I did not attend my first teachers' convention until I was twenty-one years old.

I have been a performer my entire life. My teaching specialty is music education, so even my teaching is performance oriented. I am constantly preparing students for performances or performing music or magic myself.

For many years, the music and the magic were kept separate from one another. Magic was something I did to take a break and get my mind off teaching for a while. I worked so hard to keep these two facets of my life separate that I refused to include music in my magic shows for fear that it would "remind me of work." I was sure that music was not necessary for magic and that magic and entertaining had absolutely nothing to do with teaching.

I was wrong. *Very* wrong.

THE BIG IDEA: MY "AHA" MOMENTS

In my career as a teacher, dozens of new educational initiatives have come and gone with the various politicians that pledged to "fix" our public school system. None, however, has had a greater impact on the actual day-to-day operation of schools and classrooms than President George W. Bush's No Child Left Behind Act (NCLB). It required that teachers and school districts be held accountable for their students' learning and that all students achieve to a minimum level. It set strict benchmarks for achievement and penalties for failure to achieve them.

Never before in my career has the law required such accountability from teachers and schools to improve and to reach every student. While the law is up for review and Common Core Standards may take over and change some of NCLB's benchmarks, the concepts of holding teachers and schools accountable for reaching every student seem to be here to stay. This is a monumental shift in thinking from the old philosophy that some students just don't have what it takes to be successful in school and there is nothing that teachers or schools can do to change it.

That old philosophy always bothered me. While it is obviously true that some students have natural academic talents and gifts and other students do not, I don't believe that any parent is willing to accept the idea that their child cannot be taught and is just not worth the effort.

So, really, I like the concept of leaving no child behind. But how do we do it? How can a teacher reach a student who does not seem to *want* to be reached? That is the real problem. That is the puzzle.

Well, part of my job as an educator is to solve problems. And I like puzzles. So I have spent a considerable amount of time trying to understand the problem and work out a solution. It is just my nature. It has never been enough for me to just know the answer. I also have to understand the reasons *why*.

While working on the NCLB puzzle, I was also continuing work on understanding another issue that, at the time, I believed to be unrelated. Kids were quitting my band because they said they were bored. What puzzled me was that these were not the advanced students who had to wait on others in the group to reach their level. These were the ones who were struggling. I could not figure out how a student could be bored with something they couldn't yet even accomplish. Boredom came from repetition. When *I* had trouble understanding something, I just read more, worked harder, or asked for help until I got it.

That was where I had it wrong. I was working with *my* definition of "bored." I needed to understand *their* definition. Kids define the word "bored" differently than teachers do.

The dictionary defines "bored" as "wearied by dullness or repetition." This is how teachers think of the word. Teachers connect the word to things like long faculty meetings. The dictionary also says that an antonym of "bored" is "amused." I'll come back to that idea in a moment.

Kids use this same definition—though they think of teachers droning on rather than administrators—but there is another kid definition too. Kids get "bored" by the teacher definition when the teacher drones on about things that do not interest them. Kids also get "bored" by the teacher definition when the teacher is covering concepts they already know.

Kids get "bored" by *their* definition when they decide that something is too difficult for them. When students do not understand something, or it is more difficult than they thought it would be or than they think it should be, they give up trying and decide to be "bored" instead.

Understanding the "kid" definition and use of the word took me a long time. True to personal form, I kept working to understand until I finally figured it out. Not just the *what* of the definition, but the *why* of the definition as well. For kids, "bored" is a defense mechanism. It's one that they *need*. Adults forget about it, because they don't need it any more.

Adults understand that they have great talents in certain areas and not so much in others. They also understand that this is true for every adult. Because of this, it is not a big deal to have a problem with something and to need help. Most adults have found their talents. They don't mind not being good at everything because they have found *something* at which they are *very* good. That talent serves as their "comfort zone" and the basis of their self-image.

Kids have not found their talent yet. And even those who *have* discovered their talent have not had the time to develop it enough to be comfortable in their mastery of that area. Since they have not yet developed a "comfort zone," every failure—or even *potential* failure—is a potential humiliation, a potential reason for lack of acceptance by their peers, and a potential reason for peers to pick on them. In other words, every potential failure is a serious threat to their fragile self-image.

"Bored" protects kids from this danger. Saying something is "boring" gives them an excuse to look dazed and confused, to give up, or to quit without losing face. "I didn't do my homework because math is boring" makes them sound cool. They are too good or too cool to have to pay attention. On the other hand, "I didn't do my homework because I am too stupid to understand how it works" does not make them sound cool at all.

This last definition will even *create* "boredom" that fits the adult definition. They don't understand, so they give up and stop paying attention. This gives them nothing to do, so they are bored by the adult definition. Of course, since they weren't paying attention, they understand less, so they give up and stop paying attention sooner, so they understand less, so they give up sooner, so . . .

Understanding "bored" and its effect on attention and learning made me understand that I was not working on two separate puzzles at all. The way to ensure that No Child is Left Behind is to see that No Child is Left *Bored*—by our definition *or* by theirs. Because "bored," by any definition, leads to failure—for both the student, who fails to understand, *and* for the teacher, who fails to reach the student and help him or her learn.

This brought me back to the dictionary. And to a personal "aha" moment. The *opposite* of "bored" is "amused" . . . or, perhaps, "entertained." So the way to avoid student "boredom" is to find a way to keep them "amused" and "entertained" while still teaching the lesson.

Aha!

I began to reread my magic and entertainment books thinking of lesson plans instead of magic shows. The more I read, the more excited I got. This could really work! So I tried it. And it worked incredibly well. The "aha" grew.

As my own children grew and family expenses grew with them, I started looking for ways to book more magic shows to supplement my teaching income. Again, true to personal form, I started reading and looking for answers to my questions about how I could accomplish this. I read books on marketing and sales.

In my reading, I came across a book that explored the psychology of marketing. The author referred to marketers using the term "compliance professionals." In support of this term, he went on to explain that these were not just the people who convinced us to buy a certain brand of shampoo or a bigger television. They were also the people who convinced us to brush our teeth, see our doctor regularly, eat well, exercise, recycle, and so on.

The job of a compliance professional is to convince people to do things that they might not otherwise do—even things that are good for them.

Wait a minute . . .

This sounds like a description of teaching!

AHA!!!

INTRODUCTION

Teachers are rigorously trained in their subject matter, educational theories, lesson planning, evaluation techniques, and more, but there is one element that has long been missing from teacher training: how to get students to pay attention. The most beautifully designed and perfectly presented lesson will be useless if the students are not listening.

Getting and maintaining student attention is becoming harder and harder. Today's students are part of a culture of constant and massive stimuli and of instant gratification. A single teacher is hardly a match for the constant flow of video games, YouTube, Facebook posts, and other media that are never further than a telephone away. A smart board is cool, but even that will not command student attention for long. The novelty wears off, and students revert to the status quo—boredom—and a student who is bored *cannot* learn.

To truly teach every student, to truly leave no child behind, teachers must find a way to create a classroom where students are *never* bored, where students are the *opposite* of bored: where students are *entertained*!

Here, you will learn the skills you need to create such a classroom. I will take you step by step through the processes used by entertainers to ensure that they get and keep the attention of their audiences and how to apply these same techniques to your classroom.

By the end of this book you will understand how a personal weakness can become a teaching strength; why the pace of your lessons is likely getting in

Figure I.I. By Cathy Klasek

the way of their effectiveness; how the classic bell curve affects much more than grades; how learning about commercials and car sales can improve your classroom atmosphere; what education has to do with pets; why you need a secret identity; and more.

The purpose of this book is to introduce teachers to the methods and techniques used by entertainers to hold the attention of their audience throughout a performance and to show how those same techniques can be applied to a classroom setting to improve student attention and retention. With this in mind, knowledge of teaching techniques is assumed on your part but not knowledge of entertainment techniques.

The knowledge, methodology, and techniques employed by entertainers to keep their audiences entertained and enthralled in a performance are explained, and some of their potential applications to the classroom are given. Details of entertainment techniques are provided. Details of classroom applications are not.

Each teacher and each classroom is unique. The most effective ways to use any new technique or plan in a classroom must be devised by the

INTRODUCTION

teacher—the education professional who understands the details that make up the landscape of each individual teaching situation.

Just as each entertainer follows a different path to entertain their target audience in a way that is personal and engaging, each teacher must find the combination of techniques and methods that will best fit his or her own personality and target audience (students).

Entertainers go to great lengths to get and hold the attention of their audiences and have many methods and processes to help them create and perfect the performances they present. Each process adds to the entertainment value of a performance.

Likewise, each of the methods and techniques explained here, when incorporated into your classroom, will add entertainment value to your lessons. (In other words, your lessons will better hold the attention of your students.) The more techniques you use the more entertaining (attention holding) your lessons will be, but each idea will help on its own.

For this reason, this book has been designed so that you can read, experiment with, and implement ideas one at a time. In this way, you can explore the world of the entertainer a little at a time. You can see how each new idea affects your classroom and your students, and you can find the best application of each for your individual situation.

The book is divided into five parts. Each deals with a broad idea important to an entertainer and applicable to your classroom. Chapters within each part deal with more specific topics, and subheadings go into still more detail. In this way, you can easily find and read (or reread) any section that you wish.

This is not a book of lesson plans. It is a book of ideas—ideas that can help to create new and improved teachers who constantly engage their students; ideas that can make lessons memorable; ideas that set the stage for students to make good choices; and ideas that can create a classroom where no child is left bored ever again.

The ideas presented here are intended to spark your imagination and creativity. So take the time to think about them. Imagine. Be creative. Try things. Then try other things. Find what works for you.

While all the ideas presented *can* work together, they do not *have* to. Take one or two. Try them out and play with them a bit before you move on to the next. In other words, take your time reading. Don't rush to the end. There is no final solution on the last page. I will help you along the path, but the answers are different for each individual.

So how does the story end? The way that works best for you and your classes. Ralph Waldo Emerson said it best: "Life is a journey, not a destination." Enjoy the journey!

I

ENTERTAINING

❶
ATTENTION, PLEASE!

When there are multiple teachers of the same grade or subject in a school, there is almost always one teacher every student hopes to have. There is also almost always one teacher who is requested by most parents: one teacher whose class every student wants to be in and one teacher whose class every parent wants their child to be in.

Likewise, there is often one teacher all the students dread. There is also often one teacher the parents hope their children avoid. The reasons are predictable and easy to understand. The students want to be in the class of the teacher who has a reputation for being fun. They want to avoid the one who is not fun. The parents want their child in the class of the teacher who has a reputation for being the most talented, the teacher whose students learn the most. They want to keep their children away from the teachers who have less talent for teaching.

What is not so easy to understand is that the parents and students nearly always agree. The teacher the students hope for is the same teacher their parents request. The teacher seen by the parents as being most effective is the same teacher seen by the students as being the most fun. Why? What makes the good teacher fun? Or maybe a better question is, What makes the fun teacher good? The answer is stunningly simple.

Every effective teacher is part entertainer—not necessarily a singer, dancer, juggler, actor, or magician but an entertainer nonetheless. Some of the best do not even realize that they *are* entertaining their students. This

Figure 1.1. By Cathy Klasek

does not make it any less true that they entertain as they teach. In fact, it is absolutely essential.

To understand the reason it is so essential for teachers to be part entertainer, let's return to the dictionary. "Entertain" is defined as "to hold attention pleasantly or agreeably."

Multiple studies by cognitive scientists have proven (even though teachers already know it) that attention is necessary for learning to take place. We cannot hope to educate our children if we cannot hold their attention through the lessons. Therefore, since the law does not allow us to hold students' attention by "disagreeable" methods, we cannot hope to *educate* our children if we cannot *entertain* them through (and *with*) the lessons.

Take a moment to travel back in time. Think of one of your favorite teachers from your past, one whose class you always looked forward to and could not wait to attend. Now think of *why* that teacher's class was so special. What was it about the class that made you want to be there on a daily basis?

Exact answers to this question will vary greatly, but they will all boil down to one simple idea. For whatever reason, the class was *fun*. You *enjoyed* your time in that class. You *liked* it. The teacher held your attention, and you enjoyed the process. In other words, the teacher *entertained* you!

If you ask teachers why they decided to teach, you will hear different stories from each of them. However, if you listen closely and the story is complete, you will find that there is nearly always a common thread.

Somewhere in the history of each teacher is one of *their* teachers that inspired them and changed their life in some way. They decided to become a teacher, at least in part, to be able to make a difference in another child's life the way someone did for them.

Think about your own history and the teacher or teachers who made that difference in your life. Did the teacher who inspired you hold your attention? Did you enjoy your time in that class? Of course the answer to both those questions will be "yes." A teacher cannot inspire without gaining and holding the attention of the students. So, by definition, a teacher cannot inspire, or teach, without *entertaining*!

Entertaining is the *key* to education. You cannot educate a student whose attention you do not hold. You cannot educate a student whom you do not *entertain*!

Entertaining your students does not mean that you need to sing, dance, juggle, do magic tricks, or anything like that—though you will find as you read that all of those activities can help you to raise student attention and achievement if you have the talents to do them. It simply refers to holding your students' attention.

You already do this. You already hold students' attention and teach them. You are *already* part teacher and part entertainer. So why are you reading this?

Understanding that you must entertain your students (hold their attention) as you teach them is only the beginning of the journey that must be taken for this knowledge to actually help to improve your lessons. You must learn to *think like* an entertainer.

Entertaining, like anything else, is a skill that can be learned and honed through study and practice. The purpose of this book is to introduce you to the processes used by entertainers to develop performances that capture and hold the attention of their audiences. These same techniques can be used by teachers to develop lessons that are equally commanding of their students' attention.

Scores of books on education techniques can help you design lessons that students can understand—*if* they are paying attention. Getting and holding that attention requires knowing how to entertain. *That* is the purpose of *this* book.

YOUR COMPETITION

You already know that students spend a lot more time out of your class than they do in your class. You have to deal with these outside influences in your classroom on a daily basis. You need to work to change the effect of some of these influences—for example, lack of responsibility, social skills, or motivation to learn and succeed—but you can't possibly change them all.

You must choose your battles. Work to change the effects of the influences that are most destructive to the futures of your students and that you can potentially change. The ones that are not such a big deal and the ones you have no chance of changing need to be left alone.

Alcoholics Anonymous sums up this idea in their official prayer: "God, grant me serenity to accept the things I cannot change, courage to change the things I can, and wisdom to know the difference." This is a wonderful philosophy to incorporate into your educational thinking. Whether or not you use it as a prayer, **use it as a teacher**. This idea is mirrored in a saying that was once printed on coffee cups marketed to music teachers: "Never try to teach a pig to sing—it wastes your time and annoys the pig." Stop trying to change things that can't be changed. It is a waste of your time and effort. Instead, spend your energies working to change the things that *can* be changed, such as the knowledge and attitudes of our students.

Our children are constantly bombarded with media. When they go home, they are watching TV, playing video games, and surfing the Internet. You cannot change this. Don't try. Instead, accept it as fact and adapt your teaching to work with this truth rather than against it. In other words, if you can't beat 'em, join 'em.

Adapting will not be easy. You have stiff competition. You are up against Phineas and Ferb. You are up against YouTube. You are up against Angry Birds.

The only way to adapt and keep up with this type of competition is to put on your own show. Again, this does not mean singing, dancing, juggling, ventriloquism, magic, or the like. It means you. Your show. Your **education** show. The show is not the classroom. The show is not the lesson. It is not the book. It is not the subject. It's **you**. Students will learn or not because of **you**: who you are and how you present your lessons. They will learn because **you** make them want to. They will remember because **you** made it memorable. In other words, they will learn and remember because **you entertain them**.

WORK VERSUS FUN? MOTIVATION TO LEARN

There are teachers who will say that learning is hard work and should not be about fun. This statement is only partly true. If "hard work" means "effort and attention," then yes, learning takes hard work on the part of the student. Agreed.

The "no fun" concept, however, is completely false. No student will expend the effort necessary to master new concepts without motivation. And let's face it, fun is more motivating than no fun.

Some students are self-motivated. They will do the work without motivation from the teacher. They have a personal desire to learn or to please their parents or their teachers with their accomplishments. These are the students that teachers often point to when saying that fun is not necessary for education. Unfortunately, this is also the group of students that could get along almost as well without a teacher. Self-motivated students will learn because of their personal drive and desire to learn—with or without a teacher.

The students that really *need* teachers are the ones who need motivation to learn. Students who need extra help academically also need to have a goal, an incentive, *motivation*. Regardless of the reasons for a student's lack of focus on schoolwork, it is the teacher's job to provide a reason for the student to spend the time and effort necessary to learn. Without the proper motivation, no teaching method is effective. What difference does your presentation of a lesson make if your students do not pay attention?

This brings us back to the idea of adding fun to lessons. The point here is not to say that school should be nothing more than a big party. School should be about learning more than it is about fun, but that does not mean that teachers can't make the learning enjoyable, engaging, or at least pleasant. Teachers who are able to make learning enjoyable and engaging are, in part, entertainers. They are also incredibly effective educators.

ENTERTAINING LESSONS: TIME WASTERS OR TIME SAVERS?

One of the first arguments a teacher will offer against the idea of incorporating elements of entertainment into their lessons is the limited amount of teaching time available. With the rigors of mandatory standardized testing; financial penalties for failure to meet benchmarks for No Child Left Behind's (NCLB) Adequate Yearly Progress; the coming necessity to prove student improvement through the implementation of Common Core Standards; and the accompanying performance-based evaluations for teachers, it is easy to understand why teachers would not want to give up even a moment of their precious instructional time to add "fluff" to their lessons.

Teaching loads seem to be constantly on the rise, and teaching time never increases to match. As a matter of fact, mandatory testing gives teachers *less* time to teach new concepts. Between the time necessary for test-specific preparations and the time necessary to administer the tests—as well as, of course, the inevitable make-up tests to follow—teachers have lost literally *days* from their previously available teaching time.

There is no time to waste. This is *exactly* why we need to incorporate the fundamentals of entertainment into our lessons. Adding entertainment value to our lessons is not a time waster. It is an incredible time *saver*!

An entertaining lesson does not have to be any longer than a boring lesson. It just has to be structured differently. In fact, lessons structured from an entertainer's point of view often move faster than their counterparts.

If students are entertained through the lesson, their minds won't wander. They will focus on the lesson. There will be less distraction and less need to explain an idea more than once. Because of this, they will learn faster.

But wait—there is more! Entertaining lessons don't just move faster than the old lessons; they are also retained by the students better.

Children have amazing capacities for learning. They can recount the plots of their favorite television shows in detail after a single viewing. They can recite the lyrics from the newest hit songs after only a couple of hearings. They can produce incredible lists of facts about their favorite singers, actors, sports figures, video games, and so on. Why can they remember these things so easily? They relate to the students' interests. They are subjects that the students find *entertaining*.

How much of your time is spent reviewing, reexplaining, and reteaching concepts that students failed to understand the first time or forgot since they were last covered? Is the opportunity to save some of the instructional time and effort spent reteaching worth your time to design entertaining lessons?

2

ANATOMY OF CHARACTER

The word "character" will be used throughout this book. The dictionary and common usage leave this word open to interpretation. In the world of education, the word "character" can have different meanings. Sometimes teachers will describe a very spirited student as being "a real character." Many schools have "Character Counts" programs wherein they try to teach positive personal and interpersonal skills. While both of these are perfectly valid uses of the word, neither is the definition used for the purposes of this book.

The definition of the word "character," as it is used in this book, comes from the theater. There, the word refers to personality types, distinctive traits, and mannerisms that make an individual unique. In the formation of a theatrical character, these traits and mannerisms are usually exaggerated for dramatic effect.

This is the type of character created, developed, and used by entertainers of all types. All entertainers employ this type of character when on stage. Audiences do not want to see regular people on stage. They want to see exceptional people with exceptional traits and abilities. They want to see *characters*.

This is also the type of character that can and *should* be created, developed, and used by all teachers, and for good reason.

To your students you are not a person. You are a teacher. It's different. Students do not see you the same way they see other adults. You are a different breed. You are more than human. You are kind of a superhero.

This is why students are surprised to see you at the grocery store, in the mall, or at a movie. They don't think of you as regular person. They don't think of you doing the same things other people do. You can't possibly be a regular, mild-mannered person. You have more knowledge and ability than even Mom and Dad. You are Superteacher!

Not even comic book superheroes can be super all the time. They have a mild-mannered secret persona (character) that they put on to allow them to be a regular person and do normal things. Teachers need that ability to release themselves from the rigors of their jobs as well.

Since you, most likely, were not born with comic book superpowers, you don't have to create a mild-mannered, regular-person persona. You *are* a regular person. Instead, create a *teacher* persona that *does* have superpowers—not comic book powers but super*teacher* powers. Create a character who is *always* positive, happy, and enthusiastic; a character who is caring, firm, and fair; a character whose lessons are always engaging and entertaining; and a character who shares and instills a passion for learning in all students.

We all have bad days from time to time. As much as we try to avoid it, our bad days often affect our teaching and our students. While it is absolutely normal and human for this to happen from time to time, it is not fair to our students.

To put it bluntly, your students don't care if you are having a good day or if you feel well, and they shouldn't. You are a teacher—a superhuman. The students expect you to be consistent every day. The students *need* you to be consistent every day, no matter how you feel or what is going on in your personal life.

A normal person can't possibly accomplish this. Only a superpowered superteacher can hope to live up to this standard.

Since you are almost certainly a normal human being, there is only one way to live up to the superteacher expectation: become an actor—or at least learn to think like one. Create a character that can do all these things and more. A lot of your character's traits and qualities will probably be an extension of your normal self. Take your best teacher traits and turn them up a bit. Make your character more enthusiastic, more caring, more consistent, and more entertaining than your normal self. Amplify and magnify your best teacher qualities. Create a personality caricature.

A caricature is a drawing that intentionally exaggerates physical qualities or characteristics for comic effect. Jay Leno might be drawn with a chin larger than the rest of his head. Barack Obama might be drawn with absurdly large teeth and ears. The hard part of drawing these images is to distort and exaggerate enough to make the drawing funny but not so much as to make the subject unrecognizable.

Do this with your personality traits. In the areas you feel strongest as a teacher, be yourself—but more so. Do you get excited when a student catches on to a new idea? Get more excited—not "running around the room, jumping up and down, and screaming" excited but more excited than normal—and make sure it shows. Remember that your goal in exaggerating your personal characteristics is to be more effective as a teacher and more engaging to your students—not (necessarily) to be funny. Also bear in mind that, as with the drawn caricature, too much exaggeration can make you unrecognizable to your students.

How much exaggeration is enough? How much is too much? These questions can only be answered through experimenting. How much you can exaggerate (amplify or turn up) any particular quality or characteristic depends on who you are and where the characteristic started. This topic will be covered in more detail in the section on "Creating Your Character" later in this chapter.

Developing a teacher character becomes even more useful when you look at your personal teaching weaknesses. Your character can be good at things that are difficult for you. If you are shy, make your character outgoing. If you are insecure, fill your character with confidence. Take the areas you are weak in and make them strengths for your teacher character. You can create a character that has all your strengths but more so and one that has none of your weaknesses. The character is you but better. Play this character in your classroom. The more you practice playing your character, the more you will develop the character, and the more you will find that the character starts to take on a life of its own. It will become a part of you. You will be able to become the character when you enter your classroom and become yourself again when it is time to go home.

Figure 2.1. By Cathy Klasek

A teacher is much more than an actor or a character and, for most teachers, teaching is not so much a career choice as a way of life. Your character will always be a part of you, and you will always be a part of the character you create, so you and your superteacher will never be totally separate, but the creation of a teaching character can, to a large extent, help to insulate your personal life from the pressures and stresses that can come with teaching and vice versa.

Through the development of your own teaching character, you can learn to create enough separation that your students will not know when you are not feeling well or are facing personal problems. This separation will also allow you to leave the lion's share of your teaching and school-related concerns at school so that you can enjoy your time at home with your friends and family even after a bad day at school.

Creating a character does not mean becoming a clone of someone else. No two characters can ever be completely alike. Even actors portraying the exact same character end up portraying that character with at least a few differences. This is because each character is, in part, a reflection of the person who created it. All entertainers create characters, but each one is different. It is the differences in the characters that make them unique and interesting.

Stand-up comics each create a character that is their stage persona. While each comic strives to make us laugh, they choose very different paths toward that goal. What makes each comic memorable to us as an audience and effective at making us laugh is their individual differences, their *char-acter*istics.

Some aspiring comics will try to copy the style and stage persona of a successful comic who came before them. This never works because they are seen as a copy—a counterfeit—and the audience focuses on the lack of a genuine character rather than the material being presented. The only path to success in comedy, or *any* type of performance, begins with the creation of a unique and genuine stage character to which an audience can relate.

The same principle applies to teachers. It is the reason that "turnkey" education books filled with ready-to-use lesson plans don't work well for most teachers. The books and their lessons are built around the *character* of the author. The lessons work for and with the *character* of the author.

Without a doubt, the lessons included are wildly effective for the teacher who created them. It is, however, equally certain that the lessons will *not* be as effective for you unless you **adapt** them to *your* character. Attempting to copy the character and persona of another teacher will come across to students as unauthentic and, worse, will undermine the validity of your own character.

ANATOMY OF CHARACTER

Your character, because it will be created by you and based on you, will be an individual unlike any other. Your teacher character will not be an exact copy of any other teacher. You can base parts of your character on teachers you know and admire. (Actually, this is a really good idea.) You cannot, however, totally copy another teacher.

You are an individual. Your teacher character must also be an individual. You can take inspiration from other teachers that you admire and who have established routines that work for them, but you must eventually adapt everything to fit your own character's personality comfortably. Your character must reflect a part of you. Everything your character does must fit into that reflection.

CREATING YOUR CHARACTER

Creating a character is not an easy task. It will take time, effort, research, and experimentation to find and develop your teacher character and to implement it consistently. Your first efforts are likely to need a good deal of revision and refinement to be effective. Some are likely to be complete failures. This is absolutely normal. Keep at it. You can learn as much or more from a failure than you can from a success. Don't give up. The end result is completely worth the effort.

Figure 2.2. By Cathy Klasek

Begin with some self-examination. Make a list of the qualities (traits or characteristics) you have that you think contribute to your effectiveness as a teacher. Your list may contain items like "fairness," "optimism," "patience," "kindness," "excitement for learning," "personal concern for students," "compassion," and "attention to detail." Look over the list for qualities that might be even more effective if you "turned them up" or exaggerated them a bit, as with the caricature discussed in the previous section. (This will likely be most, if not all, of your list.)

List some things you can do to display these exaggerated characteristics. If you were a person who was *more* optimistic than even you *are*, how would you behave? If you got even *more* excited about the presentation of a lesson, what would you do?

If this takes you a bit out of your comfort zone, good! Growth rarely happens completely inside your comfort zone. Besides, *you* are not going to be the one to do these things. It will be your *character* taking the risks.

Next is experimentation time. Teach a lesson or two "in character" using just one or two of these exaggerated characteristics. See how you and your students react. After the lesson, reflect on the effectiveness of the character with the qualities you were working with. Think about how the new or exaggerated qualities of your character affected student attentiveness and retention. Think about how they fit in with the rest of your own characteristics and those of the character you would like to create.

Some qualities you experiment with will be effective right away, some will need modification, and some just will not work with or for your character, but the only way to find out which ones are which is to try them out. Think about how each quality or characteristic could be changed or tweaked to be more effective, and experiment again.

Once you find the right level of exaggeration for your character and the traits you are working on, practice. Continue to teach using your newly exaggerated traits. Over time, the exaggerations will begin to feel comfortable and natural to you and your character. Displaying them will require less thought and effort.

When you become comfortable with one or two exaggerated qualities in your new teacher character, go back to your list and choose another. Experiment with combinations of traits and amounts of exaggeration to find what fits your new character best. Successful combinations should be engaging and entertaining for your students and at least somewhat comfortable for you. (Your comfort level with your character's qualities and characteristics will grow over time.) Continue to experiment and add traits one at a time until you reach the end of your list.

Once you have become comfortable with a teaching character that is an "amplified" version of you, it is time for some research. Look around at other teachers in your school. Look at teachers in other schools. Look back at teachers from your past experiences. Think about the "perfect teacher." Make a list of the qualities they had that made them effective and enjoyable teachers. Think about which of these qualities might fit with your current teacher character. If they fit, should those qualities also be "turned up" to be more effective? If they don't fit, is there a way they could be modified so that they do?

When this new list is complete, it is time to experiment again. Take the new qualities and try them out one at a time. See how your students react to each. Keep, modify, and throw out each as they seem to work for your students and to fit your new character.

Keep in mind that this part of the process will move much more slowly than the last. You are working on adding traits to your character that you don't possess personally. This takes much more time and effort than simply "turning up" the traits you *do* possess. Be patient. Keep at it—just like you would ask a student to do when they have difficulty with a new concept or skill.

After quite a bit of thought and experimentation, you will begin to "find" your character. There will be a mix of qualities with varying degrees of exaggeration that fit together to make an incredibly effective teacher. At this point in the process, there is good news and bad news. The good news is that the hardest part is done. The bad news is that you are not finished yet.

Now that you have "found" your character through the development process, you must practice playing the part and getting into and out of character so that you can play the part consistently and convincingly. Develop the character even more fully. Search for how this new, and even more effective, teacher would handle the various situations you are faced with in the classroom. How would a teacher who is even *more* patient and fair deal with the students who frustrate you? How can you add these traits and behaviors to your new character? Each new situation you explore will result in a deeper, more complex, more effective teacher.

More good news is that the more you practice playing your new character, the easier (and more comfortable) it becomes. The character will become its own identity—sort of take on a life of its own. Your character will be incredibly effective, completely consistent, and helpful by insulating your teaching from your personal concerns, and your life at home from the pressures and stresses of teaching. You will be able to step into and out of character easily whenever the need or want should arise.

Your character will evolve over time. The evolution and change happen the most and the fastest during the initial creation process, but changes and growth can and *must* continue throughout your career. As you learn and refine your teacher's characteristics and techniques, your character will evolve and improve its effectiveness.

The process of discovering and developing your teacher character is much like the adolescent process of deciding what type of person you are going to grow up to be. You see a trait or behavior, or you have an idea; then you try it out for a while to see how it works for you. Things that you like and that work, you keep. Things that do not fit you, or that just plain don't work, are thrown out, and you start looking for something else to try in its place.

Although all teachers are told they should try to be consistent 100 percent of the time, some inconsistency is a necessary part of the growth process of your new teacher character. You need to try different ideas, behaviors, and methods to see which ones work for you. Talk with experienced and effective teachers to see how they handle the concepts and situations in which you feel weak, try their methods, and then play with variations until you find something that is comfortable and effective for you and your character.

Each time you find a new method or idea that works, you are further defining and developing your character. When this happens, your character changes and evolves. Each time you modify or tweak an old method to streamline it, to make it more effective, or to make it fit better into the personality of your character, you are further defining and developing your teaching character. In other words, your character will change and evolve. Your character will *live* and *grow*.

Many teachers are not fans of change. Changes are constantly forced upon teachers by lawmakers, and many of those changes are designed around the idea of reelection rather than the true improvement of our schools. Many teachers have been frustrated by these mandates many times through their careers.

Change for the sake of change alone is rarely a good idea. On the other hand, nothing can be improved without change. People, like plants, must either continuously grow and change or wither and die. Growth and change in people and in characters allows us to continually improve from day to day. More information on the subject of change will be presented in chapter 20.

MIRROR, MIRROR

Audiences like dynamic performers. They are more fun to watch. Entertainers are *expected* to be more dynamic than ordinary people. Because "normal" people do not perform for audiences, entertainers are expected to possess qualities and abilities beyond those of everyone else.

Teachers, too, are expected to possess qualities and abilities beyond that of average people. To be successful, they must have dynamic personalities similar to those expected of entertainers.

Entertainers work hard to project energy, intensity, and emotion to their audiences because it is the dynamic personality of the performer (or teacher) that draws and maintains audience (or student) attention. When the audience members feel this energy, they become involved in the performance and reflect that energy back toward the performer.

When a performer feels energy reflected back, he or she knows that the audience is involved and enjoying the performance. This knowledge is exciting for the performer and helps to raise the energy level of the performer even more. The heightened energy level is also felt and reflected by the audience. This cycle can continue throughout the entire performance.

Entertainers (and teachers) must understand and remember that the energy that is reflected is not as strong as the energy that is sent out. In other words, the audience (class) will reflect the energy of the performer (teacher) but at a lower level than the performer sends out. In order to create a desired level of response in an audience, the entertainer must project *more* than they expect to receive.

Classrooms work the same way. A class will reflect the teacher. The students are a mirror of their teacher (albeit a somewhat hazy mirror). In order to create student excitement about a lesson, the teacher must project excitement about the lesson. If student excitement for a lesson is to grow, teacher excitement must grow as well.

Attitudes, mannerisms, speech patterns, and more are also picked up and subconsciously mirrored. An audience that is dull and lifeless is most often a reflection of a performer who lacks a dynamic persona or has not established a connection with the audience. Since it is the performer's task to entertain the audience, only a change in the performer will correct the problem.

Likewise, a lifeless, unmotivated class is most often a reflection of a teacher who has not connected with the students, has not communicated passion for the subject or excitement in the lesson, or has not created a teaching character that is compelling and demands student attention. Only a change in the teacher's attitude, presentation, and character will be able to create a change in the atmosphere of the class.

In the movie *Ferris Beuller's Day Off*, Ben Stein has provided us with the perfect portrayal of the teacher who presents information without regard to the soporific effect has on the class. The flat, expressionless delivery of the teacher is mirrored perfectly by the class. This is one of the funniest points in the movie because nearly everyone can relate personally to the situation. Almost everyone has experienced a teacher like this and has been a part of that nearly comatose class.

Though Stein's portrayal is intended to be an exaggeration for comedic purposes, it is right on target. The ability to relate to the situation makes this a very enjoyable scene to watch, but it is obvious that the students in Stein's class are definitely *not* learning.

Understanding this concept is *extremely* important to the character development process. Your teacher character must radiate what you expect to see from your students but at a higher level. Your character must be more excited about your subject and each lesson than you expect to see returned. Every bit of energy and excitement you radiate will not be reflected in your students—but *some* of it *will*.

If, during a class or lesson, you look out onto a class that is flat and lifeless, remember that you are looking into a mirror. You have the power to change what you are seeing in your students by changing what your students are seeing in you. Ramp it up. Make yourself and the lesson so compelling that your students have no choice but to become involved.

PRIORITY ONE

As a character is developed, goals for the character must be set and priorities must be examined. (Goals for the development of the character must be set as well, but the current discussion refers to the goals and priorities that will guide the day-to-day functioning of the character—things the character wishes to accomplish.) While many of the priorities and goals of a teacher's character will differ greatly from those of characters developed for purely entertainment purposes, there is one that must be shared. It is shared by every type of entertainer because it is the most important one.

A singer's job is to sing. A dancer's job is to dance. A comedian's job is to tell jokes. While this may seem elementary and self-explanatory, it is not completely correct. The jobs of these performers listed are not their primary occupations. They are *secondary*. The *primary* job and therefore first priority of each is the same—to entertain (pleasantly hold the attention of) the audience. Anyone who performs for an audience must, first and foremost, be an entertainer. The performer must hold the attention of an audience in a pleasant or agreeable way.

No matter what medium a performer uses to entertain an audience (singing, dancing, juggling, comedy, magic, etc.), every performer shares the same main goal (first priority). The audience *must* have a good time. Their attention must be held. If an audience does not enjoy a performance, the level of talent displayed by the performer is irrelevant. Regardless of the talent, the performance, and the secondary goal, the entertainer's first job is to entertain.

The audience comes to a performance for the same reason every time—to be entertained. It is the performer's job to deliver. If the performer fails to deliver an entertaining performance (fails to hold the audience's attention), the audience will not want to return (or even stay through the end of the current performance).

A singer must sing, but if the audience members do not enjoy the singing, they will not return. A dancer must dance, but if the audience members do not enjoy the dance, the show will fail. A comedian must tell jokes, but if the audience members do not enjoy the jokes, the performance is a failure.

For entertainers, making sure the audience has a good time means the difference between working and not working. Shows that do not entertain do not draw audiences and do not make money. They are quickly closed, and the performers are out of work.

At first glance, the entertainer's first priority seems much less important for teachers. Students are required to attend classes. They *have* to show up whether they are having fun or not. The teacher will have a class and will get paid either way. So what's the big deal?

We can force students to come to class, but we can't force them to learn. Gone are the days of, "I present the information and it is up to the students whether they learn it or not." School districts, buildings, and individual teachers are being held accountable for the amount their students learn or don't learn. Federal and state funding *depends* on students' learning.

The job of educating students is much easier when the students *want* to be in class—when they *want* to learn. This is the reasoning behind the assertion that, while it is a teacher's job to educate students, that job is *secondary*. The *primary* job of the teacher is to hold the students' attention, to create an enjoyable experience of learning (to **entertain** them). Students can only learn when they are paying attention, and entertaining lessons create students who want to pay attention. If the lesson is not entertaining, the students do not want to come to class. They will come because they have to, but they will walk in prepared to be *bored* (to not *pay* attention). This makes the teacher's task of successfully educating students *much* more difficult.

A teacher who is not entertaining (does not pleasantly hold attention) will likely be met with vacant stares and wandering minds. Conversely, the more entertaining the teacher, the more likely he or she will look out onto a class of attentive and eager students. Remember the mirror?

A character (teacher) does not have to have an "act" (singing, dancing, etc.) to be entertaining. To be entertaining, a character must be real, intense, and passionate, and must connect with the audience (class). The character must have a dynamic enough personality to compel the audience to watch and to care what happens next.

To find examples of this type of character, look at television dramas. The characters in these dramas compel us to watch each episode to find out what happens next, even though none of the characters sing, dance, or tell jokes. Look for the traits (characteristics) in these characters that make them memorable or real to you. Find the reasons that you care what happens to the characters. Think about how you can apply these ideas to your own character to connect with your students better, and make sure they want to watch you to see what happens next.

3

THE POWER OF LAUGHTER

Laughter is incredible. It is infectious, yet it is also healing. It can be uncontrollable. It can make us cry or cause us embarrassment, or even pain; yet we constantly crave it.

Most teachers might recall reading of medical cases where people who have been diagnosed with terminal diseases have spent a week on the couch laughing constantly as they watched their favorite comedy movies and television shows. Following the week of laughter, they returned to their doctor to be told that their malady had disappeared or had been greatly reduced in severity.

Humor and a desire to laugh seem to be universal throughout all cultures of the world. While the methods of creating the humor can vary from one culture to another, and one person to another, there are some constants that make us all laugh. A friend, who is a comedy magician and has travelled the world performing, has said that, while humor varies from one country and culture to another, they all seem to know and understand when he says, "Let me show you a trick my uncle taught me: pull my finger."

Clearly, laughter is universal and beneficial for all humanity. The question, then, becomes, "What does this have to do with teaching?" The answer is, *everything*.

You have, no doubt, heard that one of the most effective ways of presenting a new concept to students is to break it down and present it to students in *their* terms. In other words, bringing the information to the students rather

Figure 3.1. By Cathy Klasek

than trying to bring the students to the information. This keeps the students in their comfort zone, their own world. This is totally true. It works.

To do this effectively, you need to be aware of the following statistic: children laugh an average of 450 times per day; adults laugh an average of only 15 times per day. That last point is *really* important. Read it again. I'll wait . . .

If you are going to bring new concepts to children in their world, you **must** make them laugh! Children live in a world of play and laughter. From birth, they learn through laughter and play. That does not change when they reach school age. Kids are genetically programmed for having fun. They learn by playing, and when they are done learning, they go play.

Assuming eight hours of sleep per night, 450 laughs in a day averages out to one laugh every two minutes and fifteen seconds! It is absolutely impossible for your students to make it through a day of school without laughing. They will laugh with or without you. (Or, to put it in potentially more accurate terms, they will laugh *with* you or *at* you.) If you want to control their attention through the school day, you *must* be in control of at least *some* of those laughs.

THE POWER OF LAUGHTER

If you do not provide something funny for them, they will create it for themselves. When this happens, they are definitely *not* paying attention to you or your lesson. The bottom line is, if you want to keep their attention, you *have* to make them laugh.

LEARNING TO BE FUNNY

Whether you consider yourself to be naturally hilarious, incapable of telling a joke, or somewhere in between, please read this section. Humor is often based on spontaneity, and most people view it this way. To a writer or creator of comedy, however, there is nothing spontaneous about it. Humor is a *science* that must be mastered to ensure results. To a comedy writer, there is nothing funny about the business of humor. It is quite serious. For these people, getting laughs or not means getting paid or not. They work and study very hard to ensure their success.

Consistently creating ideas that will produce laughs is the product of study and practice. If you have a natural flair for comedy, this study will help hone your skills to a razor sharp edge. If you feel that you are "comedy impaired" or not capable of making an effective joke, this study will help to correct that deficiency. You may never write for David Letterman or *Saturday Night Live*, but you *will* improve at being able to make your students laugh.

Being funny with your friends is not the same as being funny with your students. We all laugh, but we do not all laugh at the same things. To be funny to your students, you have to know what *they* think is funny. Kids at different ages laugh at different things. You need to know what is funny to kids the age of your students. This is where your research begins.

You may be able to find some books on child development with information about what kids of different ages find funny, but you will learn much more, much more easily (and often more *accurately*), by simple observation.

Watch the television shows that your students watch (the comedies, not the dramas). Most successful comedy television shows are aimed at very specific age ranges. Many are aimed at a specific age range *and* sex because, at many ages, boys and girls find different things funny. The shows are designed and written by experts in entertaining their target audience. The shows survive because they make their target audiences laugh. When the show stops being funny, it stops being watched, and it is cancelled.

The producers of comedy shows spend millions of dollars researching the effectiveness of the shows and their ability to make their audiences laugh. There is no better source of current information in comedy trends for your students than these television shows. The most popular shows are the best at making the students laugh. Ask your students what shows they watch, and check out the ones that come up the most.

When you watch the shows your students watch, look for common threads in the humor—not so much in the jokes themselves but in the way they are constructed. Look for the situation, the subject matter, and the way the punch line (the part of the joke that makes people laugh) is set up. The more often you see jokes made in the same way or on the same subject, the more you know that this is a standard humor point or style for your students. It may or may not be something that you, as an adult, find funny. That does not matter. What matters is that it is funny to your students.

Finding the jokes in the television shows couldn't be simpler. Just listen for the laugh track. These annoying canned laughs are the perfect markers for the jokes in the shows. Even though the laugh tracks are far from convincing, the producers add them because they *work*. The reason for this has to do with the "liking" marketing principle and our need to feel a sense of belonging. Part 4 of this book will expand on this idea.

If a show that your students watch presents a style of humor that just doesn't seem to fit your developing character, try another. There are thousands of different styles of and approaches to humor. Many of the shows will use different approaches. If all else fails, look to classic movies and television shows. Although your students may not think of these shows as "cool," and the humor used will not be "hip" or "edgy," most will include "classic" humor that can make just about anyone laugh.

There are plenty of other ways to learn about the kinds of things that make your students laugh. You can do some more research for the price of a library card. Read some books that are written for your students. The ones that sell best (you can find this information by reading the list of popular books listed on the websites of most online booksellers) and are checked out most (ask your librarian) are the ones that students enjoy most and will probably contain things that will make your students laugh. Again, if you are looking for them, you will find common threads in the humor: subjects and types of humor that your students will find funny.

Joke books are also written with specific age ranges in mind. Your librarian can probably point you to one or two that are checked out most often. These will be the favorites of the kids and your best sources. Joke books can be extremely helpful in several ways. Like the jokes in television shows, the jokes in the book have been written professionally and targeted at the appropriate age group. You can memorize some of the jokes and use them verbatim. If you do not want to use the jokes from the book word for word (or even if you do), you can take the basic outlines of the jokes and reword or rework them for use in your classroom. You can also look for patterns in the construction and the subject matter included in the jokes. The construction and subjects of the jokes will give you clues as to what kinds of things will make your students laugh. You can then use this information to create your own jokes for use in your classroom.

Keep in mind that the best jokes are written with care and thought. Professional comics spend a great deal of time creating and honing their routines. A change of a single word can make the difference between a great joke and a dud. Jokes are written, tested, rewritten, and retested until they receive their best reaction. Even the ad-libs, or off-the-cuff comments, made by professional comics are almost always planned and written in advance. This idea is covered in more detail in the section on ad-libs.

Another great way to find out what your students find funny is to watch them interact. Laughter is very important to kids, so if they have the chance to interact, they will certainly try to make their friends laugh. Your class clown can be a major source of frustration for you and can cause constant disruption to your lessons, but can teach you volumes about what it takes to make your students laugh.

Anything your class clown does that takes attention away from you and your lesson is something you should learn from. These are things that are very entertaining to your students and, often, things that can be incorporated into your lessons.

As you are doing this research, and learning your students' sense of humor, try things out. Some will work and some will not. This involves taking risks, but don't worry—you have a character to take all the risks, right?

Make notes about what works for you and what doesn't. These notes will help you to create more effective jokes in the future and to improve on the ones you have already written. If there is anything along the way that you are unsure about, use the most effective research method of all. Talk to your students. Ask them! If you ask your students honest questions about what kinds of things they find funny, they will tell you.

FUNNY IS AS FUNNY DOES

While humor and exactly what is funny can vary greatly from one person to another, there are some basic tenets, concepts that make people laugh. Understanding these can help you to create your own comedy. One of the biggest causes of a laugh is surprise, an unexpected turn. Most joke book–type humor is built on this. There is a setup that creates an expectation and a punch line that is a surprise turn *away* from that expectation. This type of humor is very useful in educational situations and fairly easy to incorporate. You just have to be willing to be silly.

Absurdity, which is a form of surprise, is a great source of humor, both as a stand-alone gag (something that is funny by itself and does not require a setup) and as a punch line. Stranger is better here. The more two things seem like they don't go together, the funnier it can be when you combine them. This can be terms or ideas that seem contradictory or illogical, items of vastly different size or scale, or anything else that fits the pattern of incongruity.

Exaggeration is an idea used frequently in comedy that is based on the idea of absurdity. Common objects or occurrences, when exaggerated, become absurd and, therefore, become funny. This is why clowns wear big shoes. Using exaggeration to make people laugh takes some practice. There is a "sweet spot" of exaggeration. Too little and the joke goes unnoticed. Too much is just, well, too much.

Another humor basic is something that gives us a feeling of superiority. We laugh because something happens that we are glad didn't happen to us. We feel superior. Physical humor is based on this idea. We laugh because it is someone *else* who tripped over his or her own feet or walked into a sliding glass door that was closed. This type of humor can also be useful in a classroom setting, but take care: a superiority laugh is based on the idea of making someone or something *inferior*, something to *never* do to a student.

Exaggeration can work wonders in the area of superiority-based comedy as well. An exaggerated trip over the leg of a desk or lightly bumping your toe and exaggerating how much it hurts can both be very funny. Exaggeration humor can also be used to take the heat off a student who accidentally does something to make him- or herself the target of a superiority laugh. The teacher can repeat what happened to the student in an exaggerated fashion. This puts the laugh on the teacher and saves the student the embarrassment.

Repetition is also funny. Repetition is also funny. Repetition is also funny.

Often, when something happens that makes students laugh, it is even funnier if it happens again. You can use this idea to plan laughs into your lessons any time you want. See the section on callbacks and running gags for more information about this. It is an incredibly useful tool. Why?

Repetition is funny. Repetition is funny. Repetition is funny.

One last thing to remember when it comes to funny is that less is more. Too many words can make a joke too complicated and less funny. The best jokes use a minimum of words. After comedians write a new joke, they hone it by cutting out every word that is not essential to the laugh. A shorter, cleaner, more-to-the point setup and a quicker, more direct punch line will always get a better reaction. Keep it short. Keep it simple.

TARGETS FOR HUMOR

Many jokes make something or someone the target of the laugh. The joke will make fun of someone or something. Be careful of who and what you target with your humor. *Never* make a student the target of a joke. If a joke must have a person as a target, your best bet is to make *yourself* the target of the joke.

Even a reference to "the kind of people who . . ." can create a problem if your students can make an easy connection to themselves or one or two other students in the class. Students are likely to point a joke at individuals they know whenever possible. If this is someone in your class, you have just created a golden opportunity for bullying.

Jokes can be made about things that happen in class only if you make it clear that you are laughing about something unexpected that happened and not at the person to whom it happened. Depending on the age of your students, your rapport with your class, and your experience and comfort level with humor, it can be moderately to extremely difficult to accomplish this.

The most effective method of dealing with this is to create an over-the-top caricature of the occurrence and make sure that the students are laughing at your exaggeration rather than at the original occurrence. Of course, if the funny thing happened to you or was created by you, there is no problem (more on this topic in a moment).

Don't worry that your students will think less of you if you joke about yourself. They will actually, though they will likely not say it, be impressed that you are comfortable laughing at yourself. Students may tell you that they thought a *joke* was dumb (usually after laughing at it) but will not tell you or treat you like you are *dumb* because of the joke.

THE BEST SOURCE OF HUMOR

You are your own best source for humor. We all have weaknesses. Most people downplay or avoid things they are weak at. Teachers should not do that. No, that is not quite accurate. Actually, it is your teacher *character* who should charge head on at things he or she does poorly.

A teacher who is a bad artist would likely shy away from drawing in class. If that same teacher had a well-developed and entertaining character, she would draw often. When drawing, she would *not* do her best. Instead, she would draw her *worst*. The exaggerated weakness can then be used as a point of humor. It might go like this:

> The teacher draws an unrecognizable shape on the board and tells the class that it is a dog, or a bird, or a house, or whatever it would have looked like if the teacher drew well. The class laughs—and they should. The drawing *is* funny looking. It was drawn poorly on purpose to make it look funny and get the laugh.
>
> A student raises his hand to tell the teacher that what was drawn doesn't look anything like what the teacher says it is. She agrees, erases a small part of the picture, redraws it to look much the same as it did before (or even worse), and asks if that is better. The class laughs again.
>
> After the second laugh, the teacher looks at the drawing, pauses for a moment, and says, "Sorry, that's the best I've got." The class laughs a *third* time.

From an entertainer's point of view, the show is going great. The audience (class) is involved in the show and having a wonderful time. From the teacher's point of view, things are even better: the teacher has become likeable because she has shown that she has a weakness and that it is all right. She has become likeable because she has made the students laugh, repeatedly. She has made a potentially boring subject more enjoyable by adding some fun. She now has the undivided attention of every student in the class. The ones who were paying attention before will be extra focused to avoid missing the next funny thing she will do (and she won't disappoint them). The ones who were not paying attention are watching now because everyone else laughed, and they missed it. They do not want to be left out again. Her students will now remember both the illustration and the teaching point well. "You know, that thing where the teacher made that *really bad* drawing of a dog?" "Oh, yeah!"

She has demonstrated with her behavior that she is not good at everything and that it doesn't bother her. She has shown that weaknesses are okay and that she is able to laugh about her own weaknesses. This is a behavior all teachers would like their students to mirror. Can you imagine a class where no student avoids trying something new for fear that they might fail?

Essentially, the entire process of using a weakness as the subject of humor is taking our proverbial lemons and making lemonade! Our mistakes and weaknesses make us human, help us put our classes at ease, help us get and keep student attention, make us and our subjects fun, and allow us to demonstrate how adults can handle mistakes and weaknesses.

CALLBACKS AND RUNNING GAGS

Two of the favorite devices of professional comedians and comedy writers are the callback and the running gag.

In a callback, a joke is made and then, after changing the subject and allowing some time to lapse, a reference is made back to the original joke. Often the callback is on a subject that is central to the theme of the comedian's set. The joke can then be referenced multiple times. Each callback to the original joke tends to get a bigger laugh than the one before.

Comedians love this technique because audiences tend to hang on their every word trying to anticipate the next callback. When it comes, they roar with laughter in approval. This technique of building laughs is so strong that comedians who use the technique through a set usually end with a callback line. It gives them their best bet for ending with their biggest laugh.

A running gag is quite similar, in that the same joke is made over and over. The only difference is that there is not a reference back to something else. The same joke is just repeated. The joke, which can be verbal or visual, just pops up over and over at seemingly random moments in the show. This is similarly effective at building laughs with each return. Like callbacks, running gags get audiences to give their full attention to the performer in anticipation of the next return of the joke.

A perfect example of a running gag comes from Las Vegas comedy magician Mac King. During his magic show, things disappear only to be later found in his pockets, his shoe, or some other unlikely place. During the course of the show, he occasionally finds a Fig Newton instead of the item he is searching for. Throughout the show, Fig Newtons just keep appearing. They have nothing to do with anything in the show, but every time one appears, it gets a bigger laugh than the time before.

Did you catch the important point for teachers in the descriptions of those comedy devices? Here's a hint: it doesn't have anything to do with a Fig Newton.

Use of callbacks and running gags get audiences (classrooms) to give their full *attention* to the performer (that's *you*) to make sure that they don't miss the next occurrence of the joke. Incorporating callbacks and running gags into your lessons can get your class to pay better attention!

The best part is that adding these bits of comedy to your lessons is easy! For example, if you are teaching a lesson where the same concept is referred to multiple times, you can make a joke about it the first time you mention it. Then, each time the same concept comes up in the lesson, just make, or refer to, the same joke.

For example, if you are teaching your students a lesson that includes a technical term that is difficult to pronounce, pronounce it wrong in an obviously silly way, and then correct yourself. Do this each time you come to the same term.

Don't worry that students will remember the wrong thing. They **will** remember the silly pronunciation, but they will **also** remember the correction! The laugh that comes with the silly pronunciation being repeated will cement the term in their minds. If you do this enough times with the correct age students, they will begin to correct you before you can correct yourself—and they are having so much fun correcting you that they often don't even realize they are learning!

If you like to use visual aids in your lessons, you can "find" a strange item in the container that holds the items. This could be a small green monkey, a rubber chicken, a purple teddy bear, a picture of a cat yawning, a Fig Newton, or anything that is totally random and completely unconnected to the lesson. Pull the item out, look at it, wonder out loud how it got there, put it back, and go on with the lesson.

The first time you do this, it probably won't get much of a reaction. If, however, the same item is found the next day (or later the same day) in a different box, it will get a laugh. By the time you have found the same item in random places three, four, and five times, your students will understand the joke and start looking for it—meaning they will pay closer attention to all your visual aids waiting for the next appearance of the random item.

Sometimes the random item can come out first, sometimes in the middle, and sometimes last. You could even have more than one of the same random item in the same box and bring them out at different times. Keep your students guessing when the next occurrence of the joke will be, and you will keep them paying attention so that they don't miss it.

You may be tempted to dismiss this idea because the flow of your lessons will be disrupted by the joke and the subsequent laugh. Put your mind at ease. Comedians often use these random jokes in the middle of a story about something completely different. After the laugh from the callback or running gag, they return to the story they were telling and *never* lose their audience. You have a choice: would you prefer that the flow of your lesson be interrupted by a laugh at a time and place *you* decide or by disruptions caused by students who are not paying attention at times *they* decide?

SIGHT GAGS

Not all jokes have to be verbal. In fact, some of the best ways to make students laugh do not require words at all. Sight gags are jokes that are purely visual. These can range from the classic slapstick of things like slipping on a banana peel or a pie in the face to silly actions or making funny faces.

Do not underestimate the power of visual humor. Not only can it make your students howl with laughter, but also it *requires* that they pay attention. A student whose mind is wandering may catch a verbal joke, but they will *definitely* miss the visual ones. This is a very *good* thing, because students do not like to miss a joke. When it happens (especially if it is a really good one that gets the students laughing a lot), they will take extra care to make sure that they don't miss the next one.

Sight gags are perfectly suited to a classroom setting. They are easy to do, they do not require a setup before the laugh like a verbal joke, they encourage students to keep their eyes (and, therefore, their attention) on the teacher, and they get big laughs.

The movies and television shows your students watch all include sight gags. You can learn a lot from watching these, but there are a couple of other gold mines for visual humor for those wanting to truly study the art of the sight gag.

Cartoons are a great source of visual humor. Warner Bros. and Disney cartoons contain a great deal of visual humor. Wild reactions, funny faces, and absurd props are only the beginning of the list of sight gags employed by cartoon artists. Warner director Chuck Jones was especially talented in including visual humor in cartoons. His work on Road Runner cartoons stands out especially because they contained no dialog at all. *Every* joke was visual.

Another place to look for great visual humor is in the work of actor/comedian Jim Carrey. He is a brilliant visual comedian who has made millions of dollars making people laugh through the use of funny faces, motions, and gestures. Several of his movies were built around his unique ability to make outrageous faces and to move in funny ways. These movies were very successful because of his talent and because of the power of the sight gag.

Two things must be kept in mind if the inclusion of sight gags is to have the desired effect. First, the teacher must do funny things often enough that the students understand that when they pay attention, they will be rewarded with laughter on a regular basis. Second, you must *never* repeat the sight gag for a student who missed it. They don't have to pay attention if they know that you will just repeat the joke for them.

If another student tries to copy your expression or action for the student who missed the joke the first time, it does not ruin the effect. A big part of the humor is the fact that the *teacher* did something silly. Students whose attention was wandering will still have to pay attention to see *you* do the silly things that the other students are trying to mimic.

AD-LIBBING: MAKING IT UP AS YOU GO?

No matter how experienced an entertainer is, no matter how much he or she has practiced, eventually something will go wrong during the act. Something unexpected will happen; something will not work correctly; or a momentary memory lapse will cause performers to lose their place in the act. Regardless of the details of the occurrence, Murphy's Law momentarily takes over the show. This is a moment on stage that separates the amateurs from the professionals.

When unexpected events throw a wrench in the planned performance, many amateurs just freeze. Because this is something that has never been rehearsed, they don't know what to do or say about it or how to fix it. The show grinds to a halt. After considerable embarrassment on the part of the performer, and much discomfort on the part of the audience, the performer will attempt to restart the show, but the damage has already been done.

It is very rare to see this kind of thing happen with a professional. The reason is not that they are better rehearsed than the amateur. The reason is not that they are immune from Murphy's Law or the other problems that plague the amateur. The reason *is* that the professional is better prepared than the amateur. The professional has planned for problems. But there is more to it than that. Professional performers plan for problems because they know that, at some point, something *will* go wrong. Professionals have devised methods to get through these problems before they happen. Professionals are ready to ad-lib.

The dictionary will tell you that that "ad-lib" means impromptu or without preparation. Professional entertainers define the word differently. To them, "ad-libbing" requires a great deal of preparation. It is contingency planning. They think about all the things that could possibly go wrong in a performance and then plan what they will do about them to keep the show moving forward if something should go wrong. The preparation helps but is not the true reason you will almost never see something go wrong in a professional's performance.

No matter how much advance planning and preparation has been done, something *will* eventually go wrong that was not foreseen. At times like this, a genuine and unprepared ad-lib is necessary. For the professional, this is possible because the process of planning ad-libs—ways to deal with potential problems in a show—(even those that are never used) helps in the development of a complete character.

Exploring ways a character might deal with some mishaps helps to define ways that same character would deal with anything. It is the professional's well-developed character that allows him or her to carry off a mistake like it was a planned part of the show. A completely developed character just knows what to do and say. When faced with adversity, the character takes over, solves the problem, and moves on as though everything was going according to plan. Sometimes this correction (ad-lib) goes completely unnoticed by the audience. Other times, the performer's character creates an excuse or a joke on the spot to cover the problem before moving on. These are the ad-libs that are noticed by the audience. The choice of which type of ad-lib to use is made by the performer based on the problem at hand and the character being utilized.

For the performer, having a developed character allows a certain amount of detachment, the ability to take a mental step back and view the problem from a calm perspective. This detachment changes the problem-solving question from "What should *I* do?" to "What would my *character* do?" The difference is slight but monumentally important. The performer does not become flustered at a problem on stage because it is the *character* and not the performer who makes the mistake *and* the correction.

After a show containing an unplanned problem, the performer will analyze what happened and why. This being understood, the performer will put precautions in place to see that the mistake never happens again—*and* work out a *planned* ad-lib so that the character can carry the mistake off as part of the show if it should somehow happen again anyway.

For the teacher, a strong, well-developed character can carry the same benefit. In a classroom, not everything goes exactly as planned. The teacher with a strong and well-developed character will not only carry these unplanned occurrences off easily and without losing the flow of the lesson but also often have a funny comment that is appropriate to the situation and that lets the students know that it is okay that the mistake occurred.

Teachers should treat student mistakes as outlined above. Never make a big deal out of a student mistake. Doing this can easily make a student the target of the joke. Instead, student mistakes are handled like everyday occurrences. Treat each mistake as though it has been made by one or more students every year since the beginning of time. This helps to make the student feel safe about the possibility of making mistakes in the class.

The ad-libs that carry off these mistakes as normal can fly totally under the radar of the students. If the situation is handled correctly, the students will never have any idea that something out of the ordinary ever happened.

Teacher mistakes and random occurrences such as a power flash can (and should) be treated quite differently. All (or at least most) of the students have already noticed the problem, so ignoring it is just opening the door for the students to talk about it. On the other hand, if the mistake or the problem is faced head on and used as a source of humor, the students will *not* talk about it because they don't want to miss what the *teacher* says. This is *exactly* where you want their attention to be. This is accomplished with *noticeable* ad-libs.

The noticeable ad-lib is another mark of a professional on stage. Someone from the audience will say or do something, and the performer comes up with a really funny or poignant line on the spot. The audience reaction is one of awe and appreciation that the performer could think that fast on his or her feet. The truth of the matter is that most of these "ad-lib" lines are not spontaneous at all. They are actually written and rehearsed well in advance. The performer has written, practiced, and memorized a wide variety of appropriate responses to interruptions, distractions, and other occurrences and is just waiting for a chance to use one.

When an interruption or distraction happens for which the performer is not prepared, the performer will usually either try to ignore it and go on or actually make up a response on the spot. Either way, notes are made after the show about what happened, how it was dealt with, and whether to keep the same response or come up with a better one should the situation occur again.

As a teacher developing a character, you want to do the same thing. First, try to plan for problems and distractions in each lesson and know what your character would do in these situations. What will you say or do if you are teaching a technology lesson and your computer or projector won't work? What if you drop your book and lose your page? What if one of your students burps *really loud*? Some of the things you plan for will never happen. The preparation is still valuable, though, because some things will happen that you *didn't* plan for, and your preparation will help you know what to do in those cases.

If something goes wrong that you *have* planned for, you can carry it off without a hitch by using the plan that you have prepared (and maybe even practiced), and your students will be astounded at how calm and cool you were under pressure. When something goes wrong for which you are *not* prepared and your teacher character is well developed, you will likely find that, because you *have* prepared your character to deal with other problems, adapting to and dealing with the unexpected will become easy and natural.

The preparations you make for things to go wrong (even if they never do) help to define and develop your character. As the process continues, your character will develop personality. This defined personality will help you to understand how the superteacher character you have developed should respond in any situation.

AD-LIBS AND MUSIC

Jazz musicians will often ad-lib. The musical term is "improvise," but the concept is the same. A piece of music will provide a listing of harmonies and chords used in a song, and the performer is required to perform something of their own creation. Just like a stage entertainer's ad-lib, many music listeners believe that the musicians make up their music on the spot, that they spontaneously compose the music as they perform it. Again, just like the on-stage ad-lib, this is almost never true.

Jazz musicians practice until they know which notes are in each of the chords and can perform them all with ease. They then use the notes from each chord to create musical ideas that fit with the harmony and lead them to the next chord or idea. Each idea is practiced, memorized, and practiced some more until the musicians have a huge library of musical ideas, or learned ad-libs, in their minds. When the music instructs them to improvise, they simply perform the ideas that they have practiced and memorized at the time the appropriate chord is called for.

The result sounds spontaneous but is really well rehearsed and completely planned out. Like the stage entertainer, musicians prepare for any potential situation until they can respond to any possible situation with a prepared and practiced response that still sounds spontaneous. The response is immediate—nearly instantaneous—aiding in the perception that it is performed "off the cuff."

Both musicians and stage performers keep a large library of ad-libs in their minds at all times. This allows them to be ready for anything at a moment's notice. As you begin to build your library of ad-libs for your teacher character, keep a notebook of your ideas. The notebook will help you to track problems and potential solutions. It will help you to refine your ideas and solutions over time. It will also help you to study your ideas so that you can always have them in mind, just waiting to come out in the correct situation.

STEPPING ON A LAUGH

It is very important that teachers who intend to use humor in the classroom understand that they should *never* step on a laugh. Stepping on a laugh is an entertainer's term for attempting to move on with an act too soon after the beginning of a laugh. The result of this action is never positive. When it happens, the audience misses part of the act and begins to think that this performer does not want the audience to laugh.

If you watch a top comedian perform, you will notice that there is always a pause after the punch line of a joke. The comedian will wait to continue until the laugh begins to subside. After the laugh has reached its peak and is beginning to subside, the next joke will be told. The comedian does not wait for the complete end of the laugh from the entire audience but will never try to continue through a laugh that has not reached its peak.

Teachers must follow this same rule. Once the joke is made and the students are laughing, give them time to enjoy the joke. A teacher who makes a joke and then yells at the students for laughing is sending mixed signals to the students.

The joke sends the message that learning can be fun. Stepping on the laugh, either by going on too soon or by reprimanding students for laughing, sends the message that the class should not be fun. Students faced with this dichotomy will spend their time and effort trying to figure out if they should laugh or not instead of paying attention to the lesson.

4

HECKLERS

One of the most dreaded aspects of live performance is the possibility of being heckled. Dealing with a heckler is a precarious job. Respond too lightly, and the heckler is likely to continue or even gain company. Respond too harshly, and the heckler will gain the sympathy of the audience and the performer will have a very difficult time winning them back. The show will essentially be over.

In a teacher's world, a heckler is a disruptive student, one who makes noises, speaks out of turn, showboats or clowns for attention, or otherwise distracts or disrupts a classroom or lesson. If you are going to keep your lesson entertaining and moving in a positive direction, these disruptive students must be handled quickly but fairly and as gently as possible to avoid turning the rest of the class against you.

Many books have been written about how to handle hecklers from an entertainer's point of view. The lion's share of them are of little to no use to teachers. Most entertainers encounter hecklers in comedy clubs, bars, or other venues where alcohol is being served. In these venues, it is appropriate and accepted to respond with insults and put downs to let the heckler know who is boss and put them in their place. This type of response is, of course, completely inappropriate in a school setting.

A different kind of book on the subject—and one that *can* be of use to teachers—is appropriately titled *How to Handle Hecklers* and was written by magician Keith Fields. Fields' book is different because he learned to

Figure 4.1. By Cathy Klasek

deal with disruptions as a busker, a street performer who worked for tips. He played to family audiences where alcohol was *not* served and where rudeness to an audience member could cost him not only the attention of his audience but also their tips, which were his livelihood. His responses had to be different.

Teachers must deal with interruptions (heckles) using the techniques of the family entertainer rather than those of a nightclub performer. The response must be appropriate to the type and severity of the interruption, quick enough to keep the show moving, and gentle and fair enough to keep the audience's attention focused on the show. The following are some basics of dealing with hecklers in the style of the family entertainer and the ways they apply to the classroom.

The best response to an interruption is the gentlest one that will accomplish the task of keeping the entertainer in charge of the show. If the heckle was a slight annoyance for the performer but went largely unnoticed by the audience, the best response is no response at all. If the disruption does not bother your audience (class), let it go and continue the performance (lesson).

When a response becomes necessary, the motivation for the interruption has a lot to do with how the interrupter should be handled. If the person who interrupted is just trying to include him- or herself in the fun, it is usually best to acknowledge the comment, laugh if it is funny, and go on. This gives interrupters the attention they desire for a brief moment, keeps the crowd (class) on your side, and even keeps them on topic. This works because this type of heckle is topical by nature and lends itself easily to continuing the show (lesson) as though the interruption had not happened or as though it was a planned part of the show (lesson).

When a case like this occurs in an educational setting, it is recommended that the teacher find a moment to talk with the interrupting student after the lesson is over to find out the actual cause of the interruption and to attempt to make arrangements with the student to ensure that the disruption does not happen again.

Only the most grievous and severe interruptions should be dealt with immediately. Most others will stop if they are acknowledged briefly, or ignored, depending on the type of interruption and the reason behind it. Teachers should use minimal response unless the offense is grievous or the student causing the distraction or disruption is a constant offender. Once you decide that the student or behavior has to be dealt with immediately, the best method is usually to fall back on your classroom or, if necessary, to build a discipline system. These systems are generally set up to be quick to implement with a minimum of distraction from your lesson. They are usually fairly effective as well. Stop the lesson just long enough to implement the appropriate discipline system, and then go straight back to your performance (lesson).

If you do not currently have a consistent and effective discipline system in place, there is a myriad of books available with possible solutions. Another option is to talk with other teachers who have effective classroom discipline and ask for help. Most teachers are happy to share their methods and will gladly spend the time necessary to help you understand a new system and put it in place.

PACING

The most effective method for dealing with hecklers and disruptors is to make sure they never have the desire or get the opportunity to interrupt. Most classroom interruptions occur as a result of students becoming *bored* (by either definition).

Proper lesson pacing is essential to keeping interruptions to a minimum. Please understand that this does not necessarily mean that you should move faster. To find the best pacing for your students, some teachers may need to speed up, but most will need to slow down.

Here is a scary statistic: most teachers speak at a rate of 150–200 words per minute, but most students comprehend at a rate of only 50–100 words per minute! What happens to all those extra words? They get lost in space. This is the reason you can finish a brilliant explanation of a new concept only to be met with blank stares. Your explanation was perfect, but the students did not comprehend enough to make sense out of your presentation.

At absolute best (if you speak slowly and they listen fast), your students are still only really understanding two out of every three words you say. *One-third* of your instructional efforts are wasted! At worst (if you speak quickly and they listen slowly), your students only really understand one out of every four words you say. *Three-fourths* of your efforts can be wasted here! Of course, all the students in your class understand and miss different words, so the only way to deal with the problem is to slow yourself down and repeat important points.

Think about that: students are likely missing one-third to three-fourths of what you say. The only way to deal with this is to speak more slowly and repeat yourself. The only way to deal with this is to . . . speak . . . more slowly . . . and . . . repeat . . . yourself.

> Repetition is ***** and useless **** your ***** of view, *** from a ***** point of ****, it is ****** for *******.

No, the last sentence was not written that way to edit out the dirty words. If students listen and comprehend more slowly than you speak in class—and they do—that last statement is written the way your students are likely to comprehend what you say. It is a scary thought. With this in mind, though, it is a small wonder that students don't understand your explanations the first time through.

The second time you say something, the students will still miss some of the words, but they will be *different* words. The students will also recognize that you are repeating yourself and will be able to fill in some of the blanks from the first time through. Here is the full statement:

> Repetition is boring and useless from your point of view, but from a student point of view, it is mandatory for understanding.

Get it?

Test this out for yourself. Give instructions and explanations at your normal rate of speed and watch your students' eyes for signs of understanding as you do so. During a different lesson, slow your rate of speech. Repeat instructions and explanations. Again, watch your students for signs of understanding as you do this. Vary the speed of your speech and the number of times you repeat explanations and instructions with a close eye on the level of understanding you see in students' eyes, the level of comprehension shown by student answers in assessments, and the level of student compliance to specific instructions.

With a little experimentation, you will find an optimal rate of speech (probably slower than your normal speed) and the number of repetitions necessary for your students to completely comprehend and process the things you say. Slowing your speech and repeating key phrases can actually allow you to become a more efficient teacher. Your students will understand explanations more fully the first time you go over them, and when you check for understanding, they will have the concept more quickly.

If, after you explain a concept, you check for understanding to find that many students do not yet understand, you are probably speaking too quickly. After a second explanation, you may check again to find that only a few more students have caught on. Quite often, it may take three or more times through the cycle before the class truly understands the concept. By slowing down and repeating immediately, your students are able to piece together the explanation more easily, so they most often understand at the first check. The first explanation takes a bit longer, but the method will save you two more times through the teaching cycle. You will actually be able to teach *more quickly* when you speak *more slowly*!

BRAIN OVERLOAD

Ask your students, "Have you ever been in a class where the teacher threw so much new information at you all at once that you could not possibly keep track of it all?" It is likely that you will find that the answer is almost *universally* "yes." While it is reasonably certain that the cause of the problem is the speed with which the teacher presents the material, there is a side effect of this phenomenon all teachers should be aware of: "brain overload."

It is natural and sensible to believe that when the brain becomes overloaded with input (it receives more information than it can process in the time allotted), some information will be lost and some will be retained. This, however, is not correct. When the brain becomes overloaded, it shuts down completely to allow itself time to recover. It is similar to the computer errors that cause a program (or an entire system) to shut down. The program (or system) must then be restarted before any progress can be made. From the moment the overload occurs, all the brain's resources are spent trying to recover from the excess input. During this time, no new information is processed. None. Zip. Zilch. Zero. Nada.

When a teacher races through a lesson in the last five minutes of class in order to complete the day's plan, the students' brains literally shut down. If you have ever wondered why this type of teaching is met with student eyes that are glazed over, now you know. The entire class has been overloaded. They have shut down and are attempting to restart before the bell rings. When they return to class, they will not remember *any* new information. They may not even remember that the concept was brought up.

Worse than the wasted instructional time is the possibility that the students have associated the subject you were trying to cover with the brain overload. If this happens, the students will decide that the subject is too difficult for them to understand because they had trouble with it the first time. This is very unfortunate because the problem was not with the subject. The problem was with the speed of the presentation.

5

CREATING INTEREST

The next important issue for keeping disruptions to a minimum is to keep student interest high. Students will work harder to comprehend if you are talking about something that interests them. This is easy if you are teaching a math lesson to a student who loves math. It is much more difficult if you are trying to teach a math lesson to a student who *hates* math.

Getting and maintaining student interest can sometimes be accomplished by drawing real-life parallels, explaining how the students will use the information, and creating interactive projects that require the use of the information. These methods can work but are neither foolproof nor universal.

Next time, try this entertainer's trick: connect the subject to yourself personally. It is human nature to want to get to know new people, especially teachers, presenters, authors, actors, musicians, sports figures, and the like. If you tell a story about yourself that includes the subject, your students will pay closer attention because they feel that they are getting a sneak peek into your personal life. They will remember the subject because it connects to *you* and the *story* you told.

Want to ramp it up even further? Make the story about you, but when you were *their* age. Tell them about mistakes that you made, problems you had, or things your teachers or parents said or did to you. To your students, it doesn't get any better than that. This is the backstory on the superhero: Clark Kent before he discovered his power; Peter Parker before he was bitten by the radioactive spider; you as a normal person—before you acquired your teaching superpower.

This method will almost always work with students because it gives them not only insight into your personal life and your childhood but also a potential opportunity to hear about your mistakes and missteps. Make sure you include your mistakes in the telling of the story. Including these gives your students the opportunity to laugh at you about something you did before you were as smart as you are now. Remember: *you* are the best source of and target for classroom humor, and kids *love* to laugh.

Create and maintain interest, slow your speaking pace, and repeat important points at least once. The result? Increased understanding and better retention of new topics.

Of course, not everyone reading this has a poignant, interesting, or humorous story from their present or past life that can be tied into every subject that they need to teach. This leads to an interesting conundrum that occurred when *I* was a child . . .

> I was in fourth grade. My teacher, Mrs. Thornton, gave us a writing assignment. We were to write a full-page essay detailing an event in our lives when we had been let down by someone we idolized. We were to go on to describe how we felt after being let down and how we got over it.
>
> I labored over the assignment for days. I didn't really feel like I idolized *anyone*. I was not much into sports, so no heroes there to let me down on a bad day. The only music ever played in the house was chosen by my parents, so no heroes there. I liked a couple of comic book heroes, but they weren't real people so I didn't think they counted—besides they always seemed to win. There were some television shows I liked, but again, no real people there, and it was rare that the main character did not work out his or her problem by the end of an episode.
>
> I supposed I could write about my parents. I looked up to them about as much as anybody, but they had never promised me anything big and then failed to follow through. I had never been really disappointed by them.
>
> I talked to a few of my friends about the assignment and asked what they had written. That only made things worse. All my friends had wonderful stories about all the types of heroes that I just didn't have. How could my life be so incredibly boring and uneventful in comparison to everyone I knew? I had absolutely *nothing* to write about!
>
> I asked my parents what I should do. They told me to talk to my teacher and ask for help. I had been so distraught over the assignment and not having anything to write that it had never occurred to me to simply ask the teacher for help.
>
> I went to school the next day and was about to go up to Mrs. Thornton's desk when worry started to get the better of me. "What if she laughs at me?"

CREATING INTEREST

"What if she thinks I am weird or pathetic because I don't have heroes?" "What if she tells the whole class?" "What if she tells me that not having a hero to write about means I flunk?"

I froze. I couldn't get those thoughts out of my head. And so I couldn't bring myself to ask for help.

At home that night, my parents continued to encourage me to talk to Mrs. Thornton.

The next morning (the day before the assignment was due), I finally mustered enough courage to ask Mrs. Thornton what I should do since I could not find anyone in my life to write about.

Her answer took me totally by surprise.

"Just make something up," she said. "It is just a writing assignment. I am interested in how you write and describe people and situations; I am not worried about your life story."

Because the assignment was due the next day, I had a lot of work to do. I spent the entire evening and half the night working on the essay. Though I did complete the assignment in time, the harrowing experience taught me a lesson I will never forget.

Did you catch the point of the story?
Persevere? . . . No.
Listen to your parents? . . . Nope.
Face your fears? . . . No way.
Ask for help? . . . Not even.
Make it up?!? . . . Yes!!!

That *entire* story was **totally** made up. . . . Okay, not totally. . . I *was* in fourth grade once, and there was probably an assignment to write an essay of some kind at least once during that school year. The rest? . . . Fiction.

If you read the story with interest or felt sympathy as you read it, congratulations on being a part of the human race. We all want to know about the people around us. We love to hear about the experiences of others and compare them to our own. The funny thing is that it doesn't matter if the story is true or not. What matters is that the story is engaging and believable. Books, TV shows, and movies constantly surround us with made-up stories to which we pay avid attention as though they were real. We are drawn in because the stories are engaging and believable.

If you are looking for a way to engage your students in a lesson and you do not have an appropriate story to tell from your own life, you have a couple of options. The first is to check with friends, family, and fellow teachers to see if anyone else has a story you can tell. A story about a friend is nearly as effective as a personal story.

Your second option is to simply make up your own story. This is often the most effective method. Your story can be exactly what you want or need it to be. It can be tailored to make your point perfectly.

If you are not sure that a story you made up is believable, or if you are not sure of your ability to tell the story convincingly as though it were true, present it as fiction. Fictional stories can still increase student attentiveness during a lesson. Stories the students think are about you are much more powerful, but they only work if the students believe you.

Teachers can and should tell stories often in the educational process. The stories can be true, slightly embellished, or outright fiction. They all accomplish the same purposes of increasing attention and retention and all work equally well when told with conviction.

If it fits your teacher character and the story at hand, it is best to tell every story as a true story and not point out the parts that are made up. The reason for not pointing out the fiction in stories is sound from both an educational and an entertainment standpoint.

From an entertainment standpoint, stories are written to create a "suspension of disbelief," a feeling within the audience that the story *could* be true. We, as consumers of the stories, willingly suspend our disbelief—we ignore the part of our brain that tells us that this didn't or couldn't really happen—so that we can become personally involved and engrossed in the story.

No book, TV show, or movie points out its fictional nature during the story. It would break the flow of the story and ruin the suspension of disbelief. The disclaimer that we now sometimes see about stories being fictional and not based on any real person is provided for legal reasons only (to keep people from suing) and is included as briefly as possible before the story starts or after the story is over to avoid breaking the suspension of disbelief. Any hint during the story that the characters are not real will distract the audience from the flow of the story, break the suspension of disbelief, and lose the emotional hook and audience involvement.

From an educational standpoint, you want the students focused on the content of the story and its relation to the lesson at hand. If students are aware that some of the details of the story may not be true, they will be evaluating the validity of the story rather than focusing on the content. Any distraction from the *content* of the story will undermine the effectiveness of your lesson.

Any points of fiction in your stories should be details about you personally and your experiences. Take care to make sure that these points are completely personal and believable and that they align with any other stories that you tell so that you can maintain the suspension of disbelief. If students stop believing the stories, their focus is misdirected and the usefulness of the stories is greatly diminished.

BUT ISN'T THAT . . . *LYING?*

Many teachers, after reading that last section, would ask the above question. Their next statement would be something to the effect of, "Teachers, being entrusted with the future of our youth, should *never* lie to students." True. You should never lie to your students . . . about school subject matter. You should never give students incorrect information . . . about a subject they are studying. You *can*, on the other hand, create a story to help them understand a concept. You can also make yourself the protagonist of the story in order to hold student attention. These stories are not lies. They are parables.

When you tell fictional stories about yourself, all the relevant subject information should be correct. The fictional points in the story should be about you personally. Actually, they should not be about you at all—they should be about your teacher *character*. Your character is fictional, so stories of his or her past are fictional, too.

In the course of teaching a lesson, teachers will often use objects in the room to represent concepts or other objects that they do not have at hand. They will also personify inanimate objects to help make an abstract concept more personal or more memorable for their students. By making up and telling stories about yourself, you are holding yourself up as the example. You are using yourself to personify an abstract concept. You are using yourself as a teaching prop.

So what do you do if and when a student asks if a story is really true? The answer here has to be an individual choice. Telling your students that a story is not true diminishes the educational strength of that story and any others to follow, but there is an ethical issue with responding to a direct question with a lie. A good option in this situation is to deflect the question by answering with another question such as, "You mean you don't believe me?" or, "Would I lie to you?" This allows you to change the subject and avoid answering the original question. Other possible true answers are as follows: "Maybe." "What do you think?" "It's possible . . ." "I'll never tell." Or any other response you and *your* teacher character can dream up.

6

DOES THIS RING A "BELL?"

One of the subjects covered in teacher education courses in college is the bell curve. It is also sometimes referred to as the "Normal Curve" because student IQ scores and "normal" academic abilities could be expected to fit reasonably well into this type of curved shape.

Teachers are taught that grades will normally fit into this curved shape as well. Only a few students can be expected to excel and earn an A on each assignment. A few students can also be expected to fail each assignment. Most students will normally fit into the middle of the curve: mostly Cs with some Bs and Ds on each side.

The bell curve is applied in other areas as well. When uniforms are ordered for a marching band, basketball team, football team, or other school group, current students are measured for size and uniforms are manufactured to fit them. Because the uniforms are designed to last for many years of use, extra uniforms are made as well. The sizes for these are determined by placing the sizes of the current students into a bell curve. The missing spaces in the bell curve are filled in with extra uniforms of appropriate sizes. Apparently, the size and shape of a group of people also fits the bell curve.

Tim Lautzenheiser, founder of Attitude Concepts for Today, Inc., motivational speaker, and leadership expert, has discovered another application of the curve. People's attitudes, behaviors, and leadership actions also fit the curve. This curve, however, is not symmetrical. It will lean to one side or the other based on the relative strength of the top and bottom students.

Figure 6.1. By Cathy Klasek

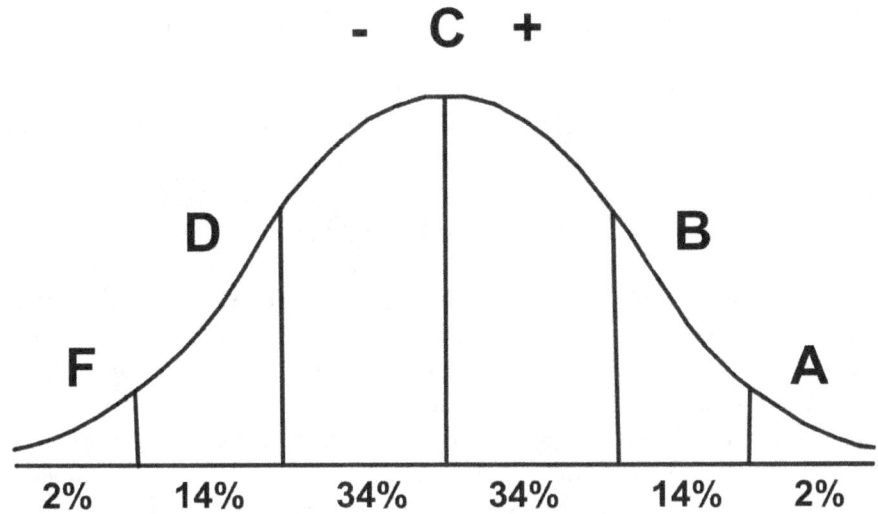

BELL CURVE

Figure 6.2. Bell Curve/Normal Curve. By Cathy Klasek

The good news is that the direction the curve leans can be influenced, and even controlled, by a teacher who understands how the process works.

Put together any group of people and you are very likely to find that about 10 percent of your group will act as positive leaders. In a classroom situation, this means that they will be attentive, be helpful, and set a good example. They will shush the talkers and scowl at anyone whose attention they see wandering. These will be your favorite students and the far right side of the bell curve.

Another 10 percent of your group will act as negative leaders. In a classroom situation, they will doodle, write notes, whisper, flip through to see what else is in the book, or even openly disrupt the class. This is the far left side of the bell curve. If you are not careful, this 10 percent of your class will take up more than 50 percent of your time.

The remaining 80 percent of your group make up the center of the curve. They may tend to lean in one direction or the other (positive or negative), but they will generally act as followers. Here is the important part: the followers will follow whichever group of leaders is more powerful.

Young teachers, especially, will occasionally have a class that is usually fairly well behaved turn on them and become suddenly almost uncontrollable. This happens because they allow the balance of power to shift from the positive leaders to the negative leaders. The followers obediently do their job and go along with the strongest leaders. In the blink of an eye, a group that was 90 percent in your favor has turned 90 percent against you.

What is most interesting about this rule is that it is true of any group. If you took the positive leaders out of each class in your school and put them all together in one room, you would find that 10 percent of them would continue to act as positive leaders, 80 percent would become quiet and look around for a group to follow, and the final 10 percent would begin to lead the group in a negative direction.

Even though everyone in the group acts as a positive leader in their own class, the dynamic of the group changes when the leaders are grouped together without the rest of their classes. Whether due to insecurity about their abilities as compared to the other leaders in the room, because they feel they must fill the void of missing behaviors, or for some other reason, you will see behavior changes in these students when they are regrouped.

This happens time and again in classroom situations. The class is poised for a perfect day because the strongest negative leader in the classroom is out sick. Shortly into the class and without warning or explanation, a student who is usually quiet and unassuming becomes disruptive. This student is usually a follower and is simply following the rule and filling the leadership void left by the absent student.

Faculty meetings work the same way. There are always those who sit in front and play "teacher's pet" through the meeting. (If you count them, it will be about 10 percent of your faculty.) There are also those who may be great teachers but who tend to sit in the back and talk with their friends or surf the Internet instead of paying attention (about the same number as the "teacher's pets" in the front, right?). The rest of the faculty sits between the two groups and occasionally looks around at the other teachers. These are the followers. They are looking around the room to see which group of leaders is stronger. This is the group they are going to follow.

You can find the same leadership patterns in every group from classrooms to governments, from think tanks to prison inmates. Random crowds are the only place you will not see this type of leadership model. There is a reason for this. The group is random—not connected. For leadership roles to emerge, the people involved have to feel that they are a part of a group. They have to feel involved or invested with the people around them. They have to share a trait, characteristic, interest, experience, or situation. They have to belong.

New York's famous Times Square is an example of this. The square is filled with random crowds of people with no connection to one another

364 days of the year. On New Year's Eve, though, the crowd is no longer random. Because the people all know that everyone in the square is there to celebrate the coming of the New Year, they share a connection. The dynamic of the group changes from that of a random crowd to that of a group or an audience.

Entertainers know this and use the group leadership dynamic to their advantage. Live performers have routines they use to "warm up" their audience. A warm-up routine is one that creates a shared experience and gives the members of the audience a sense of "we're all in this together." Once the performer has engaged and involved people in the show through a story to which they could relate, a shared participation of some kind, or a shared laugh, they stop being a crowd and become an audience.

When a crowd becomes an audience, they will think, act, and react as a group. The performer focuses on the positive leaders and gets a strong reaction. The followers react similarly, due to the strength of the positive leadership. Ninety percent of the audience is now strongly with the performer.

When put in this position, the negative leaders feel very weak. When faced with the idea that their negative feelings are so unpopular, they tend to stay silent, or even sometimes join the rest of the audience and become involved in the show to some extent. They do this because we all have a basic need to fit into the group. Everyone wants to feel accepted by peers. When faced with the other 90 percent of the audience being involved in and entertained by the show, the negative leaders will often become involved in the show as well so that they do not feel that they are being left out of the group.

Educators can use this same dynamic in the same way. By concentrating time and effort on the idea of keeping the positive leaders moving in the right direction, those students, combined with the teacher, become the most powerful leadership force in the room. The followers in the class will sense this and join the positive leaders in their involvement in the lesson or activity. When this happens consistently, the negative leaders will feel the loss of power and the loss of group membership. At this point, they will often join the rest of the class in the lesson to avoid the feeling of group rejection.

BELL CURVES AND HECKLERS

Performers always try to keep their focus on the audience's positive leaders, but they are also keenly aware of the rest of the group. Should the negative leaders be allowed to gain strength or support, the audience could easily swing in the other direction.

The leadership of the audience is from the 10 percent on each end of the spectrum, but the most powerful group in the audience hierarchy is not the leaders; it is the followers. Followers make up a whopping 80 percent of the audience. They will follow the strongest leaders in the room. If the positive leaders are not strongest, because the performer is not constantly leading them in the direction of the entertainment journey by keeping involvement and interest high, the followers will turn against the performer in a wave to follow the stronger negative leaders.

The relationship between the performer and the audience is dynamic and ever changing. Seasoned performers are aware of the nature of this relationship and keep a constant watch on the audience for signs of change. When a performer senses that an audience is beginning to lose interest or involvement in the show, he or she must do something immediately to regain what was lost or risk losing the attention entire audience to the negative leaders.

Likewise, teachers must watch their classrooms for any signs of disinterest. When these occur, something must be done immediately to regain interest or the attention of the entire class might be lost. If the correction is made when the first signs of disinterest appear, it can be a minor correction requiring minimal effort and deviation from the planned lesson. If the teacher waits to make the correction or ignores the signs of disinterest, the problem grows at staggering speeds until a major intervention is necessary to regain control of the class.

This 10-80-10 (bell curve) principle is why the handling of a heckler is such a touchy subject among entertainers. Handling an interruption poorly can lower the status of the performer in the eyes of the audience. When the performer is no longer the strongest leader in the room, that 80 percent group of followers feels sympathy for the poorly treated negative leader, giving him or her strength to pull the followers in a negative direction. If, on the other hand, the performer remains the strongest leader and remains in control of the positive leaders and the followers, then the heckler or interrupter loses sympathy and power. The heckling stops because of the disapproval of the remainder of the audience.

It is for this reason that the most practical and sage advice on dealing with hecklers and interruptions is to ignore them whenever possible. Go on with the show. Focus on the positive and make sure that you are delivering solid entertainment. If your show is good, it is likely that the heckle is not meant as an interruption but rather as a brief aside related to your show. The heckler is simply sharing his or her enjoyment of the show. Going on and focusing on the positive maintains the flow, pacing, and integrity of your show (lesson) and keeps you in charge of the positive leaders in the audience.

If the heckle (interruption) is a type that cannot be ignored, the next best option is to acknowledge the comment quickly and relatively quietly. It is possible that the interruption can add to the entertainment value of the show. Most live entertainers purposefully include lines and comments in their shows that began as heckles. This, again, maintains, at least as much as possible, the flow, pacing, and integrity of the show. Since the performer has behaved graciously toward the heckler, the followers in the audience have little reason to sympathize with the heckler and change the group of leaders they choose to follow.

The educational equivalent of a heckler could be a disruptive student or a class clown. Any student who interrupts can be considered a heckler. When these interruptions happen during your class, the attention of the rest of your class is diverted to the interrupter for a moment but swings immediately back to you to see how you are going to react. This is a test of your mettle as a teacher and a test of the effectiveness of your discipline. If you fail to react or if your redirection is too weak, the heckler will continue his or her behavior pattern. When this happens, the negative leaders gain power. The followers in the class see that the disruption had no real consequence and begin to think about following the interrupters instead of the positive leaders. However, if your response is judged by the students as too harsh, the class will sympathize with the unfairly punished student (who is a negative leader). The sympathy will translate into leadership power and the followers in your classroom will rush to the defense of their newly powerful negative leaders.

II

PUTTING A SHOW TOGETHER

7

ROUTINE (LESSON) DESIGN

This part of the book describes, in some detail, the process an entertainer goes through when designing a new routine for a show and adding the routine to the structure of a show. The process is somewhat involved, time consuming, and daunting. While lesson plans designed this way can be extremely effective, it is not necessary to go through the entire process to improve the effectiveness of your lessons.

Every part of the process outlined is intended to perform the same function: to get the entertainer to focus on every detail of a performance, evaluate its effectiveness in entertaining audiences, and improve each detail until the routine reaches its maximum impact. While the entire process is followed to create a routine that an entertainer uses time and again to create a memorable and thoroughly entertaining experience for an audience, each step, in and of itself, improves the overall product that is, for the entertainer, a routine and, for the teacher, a lesson.

At the end of this part is a chapter titled "Getting Your Feet Wet," which contains some suggestions as to good places to start incorporating the process of routine and show design into the planning and presenting of your lessons. Start with one or two ideas that appeal to you and try them out. Each one, when implemented, will improve your ability to entertain (pleasantly hold the attention of) your students.

If you find that some of the steps outlined are already a part of your lesson planning process, think about how you can improve the effectiveness of that step in the planning process, by evaluating its entertainment value, to increase your ability to hold the attention of your students.

As you become comfortable with incorporating each new idea into your teaching style and your teacher character, try adding another element. Then add another. And another . . .

START AT THE END

Entertaining routines are not designed in the order in which they are presented. The first step in designing a new routine is to define a destination for the audience. Every routine is designed, first, with a destination in mind: a mood, an idea, a surprise, or a reaction the entertainer wishes to create within the audience.

All entertainment is a journey. The audience members are taken to a place they would not otherwise have gone. They are led away from their current cares and concerns and into a world created by the entertainer/performer. Knowing the eventual goal of the routine is essential to creating the path to be followed. The entertainer is the audience's tour guide through the journey.

Every journey must have a destination. Unlike a road trip, the destination of an entertainer's routine is not necessarily a place. The destination can be a world that exists only in the mind of the entertainer, to be shared with the audience through the entertainment journey. The destination can also be a feeling or emotion. The destination can even be knowledge or understanding.

Nonfiction books, magazines, newspapers, and television news shows all share a common destination of knowledge and understanding. If you do not think of these types of media as forms of entertainment, you are not alone. Remember, though, the definition of entertainment is to hold attention pleasantly or agreeably. All media *must* be designed to hold the attention of its audience in an agreeable manner. Without this common thread of entertainment, there would be no audience.

You choose books, magazines, and newspapers that are written in a style that you enjoy. If you choose poorly, you will probably not finish reading. Many newspaper and magazine writers have followers who will read their articles every time, simply because they enjoy the writing style. When choosing a television news broadcast, you do not base your decision on the news presented (unless you know someone who will be featured in a broadcast). The amount of national versus local news they present may change

ROUTINE (LESSON) DESIGN

based on the scope of the presentation, but all news shows present essentially the same news. You choose which television news programs you watch because of the way the stories are presented and the people who write and present them. You enjoy some more than others. Some broadcasts hold your attention more agreeably than others.

Likewise, teachers should begin planning lessons by thinking about the end, that is, the goal or objective of the lesson. Without this objective or goal, the lesson will wander aimlessly. Regardless of the planned outcome, the teacher must always know both where the lesson is headed and how to tell when the class has arrived at the destination.

8

THE HOOK

Once an entertainment destination is chosen, a "hook" must be found. The audience must be enticed to follow the entertainer on the journey being created. The term "hook" is borrowed from fishing and is used in an emotional rather than a physical sense. To a fisherman, the hook is important because it is the connection to the fish. It is the piece that keeps the fish attached to the line and allows it to be reeled into the boat. To an entertainer, the hook is the statement, idea, or premise that sparks an emotional connection such as sympathy, empathy, or curiosity. The entertainer's hook, like the fisherman's, is used to create a connection with the audience by which they are enticed to follow the "line," or journey, to the intended destination. It causes audience members to be willingly "reeled in" to the intended destination.

The hook can be verbal or visual, implicit or implied. A hook can actually make use of *any* of the senses as long as it somehow entices the audience to follow along the path planned by the entertainer.

Because the hook is the doorway to audience involvement—the device used to create interest in and attention to the routine—it is always placed at the very beginning of the routine. Anything placed before the hook would be wasted, as the audience has not yet been drawn into the entertainment journey.

"Hooks" are used in television and radio news, magazines, and newspapers all the time. They serve the same purpose: to entice the consumer

Figure 8.1. By Cathy Klasek

to want to know more. The purpose of the hook is to convince the reader or listener to put forth the time and energy necessary to learn more. For radio and television news, the hook is the teaser line used before each commercial. "When we come back, we'll tell you . . ." is a teaser line. They give you a subject that will be covered soon but no detail. They are playing on your curiosity to keep you from changing channels during the commercial. Magazines and newspapers use headlines as a hook. "How to lose ten pounds in five days" and "Congress to vote on tax increase" are examples of headlines written to draw in a reader. Like the radio and television teasers, a good headline gives you a subject and just enough information to make you want to know more.

Again, teachers should follow this lead in designing their lessons. After deciding what you want your students to learn, the next most important question to answer is how you are going to create the interest necessary

THE HOOK

to make your students curious about what is coming next. Without some kind of "hook" for your lesson—some way to create interest or involvement on the part of the student—even the most brilliant of presentations will fall flat. An interesting presentation may be able to *hold* the attention of students but will be useless unless the teacher can first *get* their attention.

A hook should be designed like a news headline or teaser. It should introduce the subject and give just enough extra information to create interest, an emotional connection, or both. Curiosity is one of the most effective hooks. Asking a question, hinting at information to come, and posing a challenge that the students will be able to solve by the end of the lesson are all excellent starting points in designing an educational hook. Telling a story can be an excellent hook for a lesson. The use of humor can also serve as a lesson hook.

There are, of course, thousands more possibilities. You are limited only by your imagination and your knowledge of your students.

9

GETTING THERE IS HALF THE FUN

Now that our entertainment journey has a beginning and an end, we are ready for the third step in the design process: choosing the path by which the journey will be taken. For an entertainer, a routine is often more about the journey itself than about the destination. Entertainment happens *on the way* to the destination. Reaching the destination signals the *end* of the entertainment cycle.

    It is at this point—the designing of the path to be taken from the starting point to the end point—that teachers and entertainers generally part company in the way they make their plans. A teacher, when planning the journey to be taken in a lesson, will generally opt for the straight-line approach: the shortest distance between the two points. The material is presented in a linear, step-by-step fashion with visual aids. Some questions are asked and answered, and homework is assigned. Entertainers, on the other hand, almost *never* choose a straight-line path for their entertainment journey. The entertainer's path twists and turns through the straight-line path. The path will be straight for a short while, but at an unexpected point, the path will take a sudden turn—a twist in the plot, an aside, or a backstory—before returning to the path again.

    The twists and turns in the plot (entertainment journey) create a tension-and-release pattern that builds interest, suspense, and anticipation of the final goal. They make the destination of the journey more desirable because the trip was more interesting. Just when we think the destination is

Figure 9.1. By Cathy Klasek

in reach, a change is suddenly introduced or a problem is discovered that turns us away from the main path and must be dealt with before the destination is once again in reach.

Will we make it to the destination this time, or will we run into another unexpected problem? The only way to find out is to tune in and wait to see what happens next, and either way we are happy. The journey reaches its climax, or we meet with another exciting plot twist.

The straight-line path can still be used occasionally, either for its brevity or for variety, but most lessons should be designed with the entertainer's twisting path. This method is preferable for several reasons.

The winding path is a much more interesting one for students to follow. Because of this, you will have better student attention through the lesson.

This translates to better student understanding throughout the lesson and better student retention following the lesson.

Winding back and forth across the straight road gives you a better chance to use and apply a "hook" to the lesson. The hook does not necessarily have to relate to the lesson in an obvious way. It just has to be something to create interest in your students so that they follow the path. Starting a lesson with a hook that seems to have nothing to do with the subject at hand can be incredibly useful and powerful. It can be useful because, sometimes, finding a hook that obviously relates to a concept you are teaching is difficult. It can be powerful because it creates a mystery that the students must solve: "What in the world does *that* have to do with what we are learning?" By the end of the journey, the hook has been linked to the subject at hand and the mystery is solved. On the way, this method of incorporating a hook with an air of mystery helps to keep the students guessing as to how you will connect the topics, making another good reason to continue to pay attention.

The winding path lets you cross that straight road repeatedly so that you can emphasize and restate important points. Many students probably missed one or more important points the first (or even second or third) time through. The previous discussion of pacing provides a more detailed look into the need for this and the reasons behind it. The important point to remember here is that repeating main lesson points each time you return to the straight path will not be met with the student resistance that generally comes from repeated drilling of new concepts.

Once your lesson hook is set, start out down the straight road toward your destination. Shortly down that road, turn off onto a path to the left or right, thereby adding a twist in the plot of the lesson plan. The turn could take you into the details of a fine point of the lesson, a backstory, a joke, or anything else you can think of. At the end of the side path, return to the straight road and take the opportunity to reiterate and reinforce some of the points you made when you began down the straight road at the beginning of the lesson. Once you have returned to the straight road, travel it for a short time, until you have another opportunity to turn off onto another side path, which is followed until it leads back to the main road. This process continues until you reach your destination.

Some of the side paths should be short detours, such as a quick joke, and others can be long and winding, such as a story to reinforce a concept or simply to create or maintain interest. Each winding-side-path method gives you an opportunity to include an aside or backstory in the lesson, as they do in books and movies. This is a centuries-old model for maintaining interest and attention.

Side paths also allow opportunities to include extra detail as well as chances to make the students laugh. There is no more important or valuable tool in a teacher's toolbox for increasing student attention and retention than laughter.

Lessons with winding-path journeys can lead to topics that seem to be very far from the beaten path of the subject at hand. They can even be downright outrageous or silly. This is a good thing because these lessons are the most effective for retention. Many books on improving your memory, retention, and recall of information advocate making connections between the information to be remembered and bizarre or outrageous mental pictures. The more outrageous the picture and the more absurd the connection, the stronger your ability to recall it becomes. By making outrageous associations during a lesson, you are not only creating laughter in your classroom but also creating these types of associations in the students' minds and helping them to remember the things you are teaching.

Perhaps the best method of adding a winding path to your lessons is to tell stories. The stories can be true, embellished, or completely fictitious. They will command student attention because we all have a built-in, possibly even genetically implanted, interest in other people's experiences, successes, and failures. Besides, answering questions and teaching by telling seemingly unrelated stories was a favorite method of the most famous teacher ever to walk the earth. If the storytelling method of teaching was deemed effective by Jesus, there *must* be something to it!

All winding-path methods give you the opportunity to use the pacing lessons learned and employed by entertainers everywhere. This lesson is evident in every book (the kind written for pleasure reading, not the textbook kind) you will ever read and in every movie and television show you will ever see. No audience will follow a straight path for more than a few minutes without losing interest. Changes, surprises, tensions, and releases must happen often to maintain the interest and the attention of the audience.

The next time you read a book for pleasure or watch a movie, check out the pacing of the scene changes and the plot twists. No story progresses for long in a straight line without being interrupted by something new to maintain interest. This is the nature of entertainment and is a part of all forms of entertainment. Lessons should be planned to work within these parameters rather than against them.

FOLLOWING THE YELLOW BRICK ROAD

Step four of the entertainer's routine creation process is the actual scripting. This means sitting down at the computer and actually writing out and planning every word, every action to be used in the routine, and as much as possible, every reaction expected from the audience. This is a somewhat time-consuming step, as it involves getting up and down from the computer often. After a bit is written, it is necessary to get up and try that part with the props and the blocking to make sure that the words and actions fit together correctly; then it is time to sit down and write a bit more (or rewrite the last segment if it didn't work as intended). This process is repeated over and over until the script is finished.

During this process, the entertainer is working to create the perfect coordination of words and actions, with a consistent and logical flow to both. Both the words and the actions must somehow be interesting enough to allow the performance to command the attention of the audience.

Teachers designing lesson plans do not usually take this step quite as far as do performers when planning a routine. As a teacher, you can be less concerned about exact timing and coordination of your actions and words. An outline of the lesson is generally enough. Words must still be chosen carefully, because a change of a word or two can make the difference between understanding and confusion. Key words and phrases should be included in your lesson's "script" outline so that you can make sure to present the ideas in the most effective way possible every time.

CHAPTER 10

Figure 10.1. By Cathy Klasek

Once a routine's script is finished, the next step in the process is to practice and memorize the routine. This is a long process because the performer wants to make sure that every word and every move is just right every single time so that every audience receives the maximum entertainment value and impact possible from the routine every time it is performed. As a part of the practice process, the written script is often tweaked. A word or two will change here and there. A move or the timing of a move will change a bit. All these changes are noted in the script so that they can be tracked and memorized in the most effective version possible.

Again, when using this process to design a lesson, you can be a little less intense about the practice process. You can use your notes as a teacher, so memorizing is not necessary. It is a good idea, however, to practice the lesson before you present it. Actually standing up and going through the lesson step by step without worrying about the writing process gives you the opportunity to evaluate the flow of the lesson. Through this process, you will often notice a weak spot in a lesson. Because you are just practicing, you can correct the problem before it leads to student confusion or lack of attention.

Once the entertainer's new routine is committed to memory, the process is still not complete. At this point, the routine will be added to a show, but it is not considered finished. During the initial performances, close attention is paid to audience reactions to every detail of the routine. Quite often, the performance will be recorded (video if possible but at least audio) so that it can be reviewed later when the performer can focus on the reactions without worrying about performing the routine.

When reviewing the tapes, the first priority is to look and listen for dead spots in the routine. Any dead spots are reasons to take a new look at the script and think about what can be done to eliminate the problem. The performer needs to eliminate all dead spots because they are opportunities for the audience's attention to wander. The audience must be kept completely entertained and enthralled in the performance every moment. This delivers the maximum entertainment value for the audience and allows the performer total control over the audience for the entire show.

Most performers *hate* this part of the process. It *forces* them to notice things they do poorly. Inevitably, they will see more of these than they noticed during the actual performance, and this can be more than a little upsetting. To the performer, every error, big or small, sticks out like the proverbial sore thumb. The process of reviewing tapes, however, is essential because errors can only be corrected when they are noticed. The recordings allow performers to notice more problems, which allows them to correct more problems. As each problem is corrected, the performer is able to better control the audience and provide higher quality entertainment. The good news is that once corrections are made, the performer can watch a new tape and see the improvements.

Once the dead spots have been identified and rewrites have been completed to eliminate them, the performer will look and listen again for audience reactions to make sure that the audience is reacting the way that was envisioned as the script was written. If an expected laugh or applause point does not receive the reaction envisioned, it will be analyzed to find the reason and corrected for the next performance. This process will be continued throughout many performances until the performer is happy with the pacing of and the reactions to the routine. This is when the new routine is considered to be mature and ready to stand alone or become a trusted part of a complete show. However, even at this point, the routine is not considered complete.

When a routine reaches the point of maturity, performers will not give it the intense postperformance review given to a newer routine that is still in the development process, but the performer is always on the lookout for ways to tweak and improve the entertainment value and impact of all routines. Through the normal course of performing, unexpected things happen. Audience members may do something funny, or the performer may come up with an idea or an ad-lib that adds to the routine. When this happens, it is added to the script so that it can be included in future performances.

This can be a very useful step for teachers as well. Take a lesson you are comfortable teaching and record yourself presenting it. A video recording will give you the most information about what you are doing, but an audio recording can help a lot as well. Watch (listen to) the tape and look for weak spots. Watch yourself, but also watch the students. If or when you see their attention wandering, back up and look for what you did to allow this to happen, and look for things you can do to avoid the wandering attention in the future.

This process is one of the most powerful in terms of improving your teaching but one of the least fun. Watching yourself with the express purpose of looking for things you do poorly is *not* a good time. If you are brave enough to try this, bear in mind that every problem you recognize is one that can now be corrected. There simply is no better way to improve your teaching.

You should also keep a constant eye toward ways to improve your lessons. If during the presentation of a lesson, you (or a student) come up with a new wording or presentational twist that seems to be more effective in helping students to understand a concept, write it down! Make sure that you can use that same presentation next time so that future students can also benefit from your new discovery.

When including a new routine into a show, it is also possible that the routine will fall flat or receive much less reaction than expected. If this happens once or twice, it is not necessarily cause for concern because it can take some time for a routine to find its stride. However, when a routine falls flat consistently, it will be removed from shows and returned to the beginning of the creative process. The performer's feelings about the routine are not important. If the audience does not connect and enjoy the routine, it is removed from the show and redesigned until it can create the needed connection and reaction in the audience.

Many routines you see performed have undergone multiple back-to-the-drawing-board rewrites. Over time, the entertainer will eventually find a presentational idea that will allow him or her to use the routine as a part of a performance.

Teachers should be equally critical of their lessons. If a lesson falls flat and the students do not respond, it must be reworked from the ground up. It does not matter if you think the lesson is wonderful. If the students do not respond, the presentation *must* be changed. Eventually you will find a presentation that works and gets students to respond and understand.

This process is a great deal of work and takes quite a bit of time, but the result is a routine that can be used again and again to bring joy and wonder to audiences. For the entertainer, the result of the process makes the effort involved completely worthwhile.

This time-intensive process of routine creation and development is the *only* way to design a routine that delivers maximum entertainment value to audiences. It is the process used by all those who entertain live audiences.

Using this process to design lesson plans is also time intense. Because of the time involved, it is likely you will have the time to work on only a few of these per semester. The lessons that go through the complete process will be the strongest ones you teach, and you can build your repertoire over time.

It is also important to remember, though, that a lesson does not have to go through every step of this process to be improved. Making notes about new ideas as you teach a lesson for inclusion in the next presentation is a simple and effective way to improve the quality of your lessons. Adding a hook to the beginning of your lessons or adding a couple of twists and turns to the path of your lesson are also relatively quick and easy ways to improve the effectiveness of your lesson and to better hold the attention of your students.

IF THE SHOE FITS... TEACH IT

Each routine that an entertainer designs must fit the performing character. Everything that is performed must fit this stage character. This is the most important part of routine design. Every word that is said and every movement that is made must fit with the performance character. The character must be not only real and believable but also completely consistent throughout each routine and throughout the entire show.

Maintaining the consistency and integrity of a performing character requires some difficult choices from time to time. The choices that must be made in the establishment and definition of a performing character improve the overall quality of a show immensely, but they also create limits. There are certain things that cannot be done on stage because they simply do not fit the character.

Magicians avoid certain tricks, singers avoid certain songs, comedians avoid certain jokes, and dancers avoid certain moves because they would require things that just do not fit the performing character of that particular entertainer. A performer can watch another entertainer perform a routine that involves a beautiful presentation and completely enthralls the audience, and not be able to add it to his or her own repertoire. The performer in the audience can enjoy the experience immensely and appreciate the performance completely but know that it is effective because it fits *that* performer's character and style; it will not necessarily fit any other character.

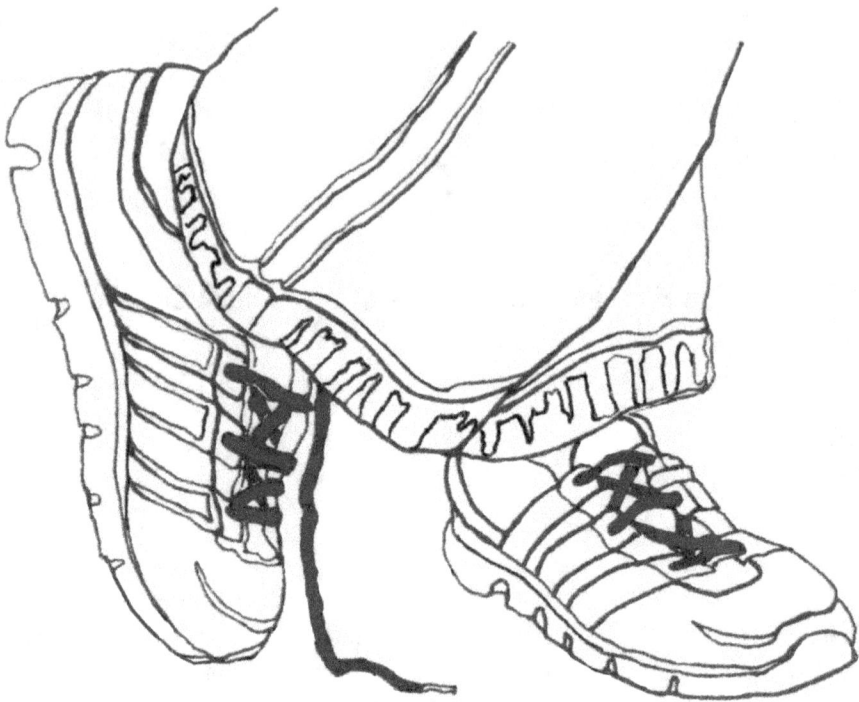

Figure 11.1. By Cathy Klasek

If a performer wants to add something similar to his or her performances, it must be worked through the development process from the beginning. If something about the original presentation doesn't fit the performer's character, the odds are not in favor of an easy or effective routine creation process.

This is true of lessons and teaching techniques as well. Although you can create a teacher character that is quite eclectic, allowing you to incorporate many different techniques and styles into your teaching, there are still some limits.

You can watch a master teacher go through a riveting and entertaining lesson that completely captivates the students, constantly entertains them, and firmly implants the required facts and skills into their memories. Unfortunately, you cannot necessarily take this lesson word for word and add it into your own lesson plans. If the other teacher's teaching character is not close in relation to your own, you cannot use the lesson—at least not in its present form. You can use the *idea* and put it through your own creative process, but you cannot use it *as is* without undermining or even destroying your teaching character.

Changing your character from one lesson to the next is confusing to your students. They understand the character you present to them on a daily basis. (Even if you have not yet developed a superteacher character, you are and always have been a character to your students because you have specific characteristics that make you who you are.) When something you do does not fit with your teaching character, the students will stop focusing on the lesson in favor of trying to figure out why you have stepped out of character (why you are acting "weird"). This is the reason that those "turnkey" (ready-to-use) lesson plans must be modified before you can effectively present them to your classes.

Each teaching character must be unique, so the methods and ideas that work for each teacher will also be unique. The more comfortable you become with your teaching character (who you are as a teacher), the more easily you will sort out what ideas will and will not work for your character in your classroom. Comfort and familiarity with your teaching character will also give you the ability to more easily adapt ideas that are workable but do not quite fit your character's individual style.

PUTTING TOGETHER A FULL SHOW

A full show is a combination of routines that are presented in an order that mirrors the winding path of the single routine. The show begins with an opening routine that is used to create enough interest that the audience members feel it is worth their time and effort to pay attention to the rest of the show. The final routine is chosen as the ultimate climax of the show, toward which all the rest of the routines build. The beginning and end of the show are connected with routines that are placed in an order that will create the desired winding path with points of tension and release, just as a movie or a book is organized.

Each routine for the show is developed individually using the process outlined previously. Each is designed to perform a specific function in the show—opener, tension creation, tension release, or closer. As each routine is created and made ready for inclusion in a show, it is included as a part of a show that is already developed until the new routine reaches maturity. It can then be rotated out of the old show and used as a building block for a new show. When enough new routines reach maturity, they can be arranged into a new full show.

As with the routine development process, the routines in the show and their order within the show is subject to change based on analysis of the flow of the show and the audience reactions.

HOW ROUTINE DEVELOPMENT RELATES TO LESSON PLANS

The same process used to create performance routines can be applied to lesson plans. The plans developed through this process will be favorites of teachers and students alike.

As with routine creation, this type of lesson planning is very time consuming. You may only have the time and energy to develop a few lesson plans per semester using this process. The process is, however, well worth the time and effort it consumes. Once these lesson plans have been fully developed, they can be reused again and again for years to come. These are the lessons that grab and hold student attention the best. The students stay focused, have fun, and retain the material covered. These are the lessons that will make you feel most like you deserve the title "superteacher."

Once multiple lessons or routines have been developed, you can combine them to create complete units. As with the process used by performers in designing shows, the lessons in the unit are designed and arranged to create a pleasant, winding pathway with different levels of intensity, with twists in the plot, and with appropriate climax points at major concepts and at the end of the unit.

A unit designed this way will not only provide your students with a mastery of the facts and concepts involved but also give them lifelong memories of how much fun they had learning new things in your classroom. It doesn't get much better than that.

⑫

GETTING YOUR FEET WET

Creating an entire lesson in the manner described in the last few chapters is a daunting task. Going through the full process is not necessary to improve your lessons. Each step in the process will improve your effectiveness and the more of the process you use, the more your lessons will improve. Sometimes, though, it can help to ease your way into an idea a bit more slowly. The following are a few ideas to allow you to "test the waters" before you "jump in."

Make your students laugh. Tell a few jokes as you teach your lessons. The jokes should be randomly placed throughout the lesson so that the students cannot predict when the next one will come. The jokes do not even have to be related to the lesson in any way (though if you can relate them to the lesson, it will improve retention). Watch your negative leaders and any students who tend not to pay attention as you do this. They will likely miss the joke, but the laughter of your positive leaders will cause them to start paying attention as they realize that they just missed something good. For maximum effect here, never repeat the joke. If you do, they know they can continue to let their minds wander and still catch all the good parts. Instead, tell them that the joke was not an important part of the lesson or point out that they wouldn't have missed it had they been paying attention.

Make weird associations or say things in funny ways. This departure from your normal routine and delivery of your lesson will cause students to pay attention (and probably make them laugh as well). If you do these things

Figure 12.1. By Cathy Klasek

consistently, the humor will stick in your students' minds, and they will automatically associate that with the information you want them to remember. They will also anticipate the next occurrence of the silliness with great joy (which will keep them focused on what you are saying).

Purposely do things wrong and let your students correct you. After you have finished explaining a concept, when you are checking for student understanding, make a statement or ask a question but get something wrong—obviously wrong—and let your students correct you. The opportunity to correct the teacher creates an incredibly empowering moment for the students. When students come into your class, they are used to you knowing everything about your subject. They are the ones who make mistakes, and you are the one who corrects them. Turning the tables gives them a huge sense of power, is a great method for review, and at the same time, creates a reason to pay attention—in case it happens again. Do this repeatedly and you have created not only a wildly successful and empowering lesson but also a running gag. Repetition of the mistake will become funnier each time it happens.

Slow down and repeat. When you are explaining an important point or giving instructions, speak at about half your normal rate of speed, giving the words time to sink in, and then repeat the explanation or instruction at the same speed. Watch your students as you do this. You will see the "light of understanding" in more eyes than normal the first time through, and even more the second.

Change your pace and volume. Too much of the same tone, speed, volume, or inflection tends to lull our minds into a stupor. Change it up. Really overdo the differences, and you will see your students look up to figure out what is going on. You have their attention now! This works for the same reason that a person who fell asleep with the television blaring will wake up if you turn off the TV. The mind gets used to consistent sounds and tunes them out. Sudden changes command attention. In the case of the sleeping couch potato, the sudden silence created by turning off the TV is deafening!

III

SELLING IT

13

HOW MUCH IS THAT LESSON IN THE WINDOW?

One part of the "aha" revelation that precipitated this book was the idea that teachers are, in fact, entertainers whether they know it or not. This led to the realization that planning and teaching lessons using ideas common to entertainers but foreign to many teachers might increase their effectiveness. This has proven to be true and has led to the first two parts of this book.

The "entertainer" revelation, powerful as it was on its own, came alongside another discovery that, when used in conjunction with entertainment knowledge, greatly increases a teacher's ability to reach *all* students with the lessons: every entertainer is also in the sales business.

Entertainers who have perfected their art have only begun. The show still needs customers—audiences who are willing to watch the show. A great show with no audience is no show at all. The show must be sold.

In today's digital age, consumers have nearly instant and unlimited access to entertainment. Why should they choose your show over all their other options? Entertainers must be able to present a convincing argument that their talent and skill—their *show*—is worth the investment of time and money necessary from the consumer. They must "sell" the audience on their show before it even begins, or there may not be a show at all.

Some famous bands, Hollywood actors, and other professional entertainers hire an agent to do this work for them. Those of us who can't afford the services of an agent must sell our own services.

Figure 13.1. By Cathy Klasek

Again, for the sake of clarity, specific definitions for the terms "selling" and "salesperson" must be established. For the purpose of this book, "salesperson" does not mean the teenage, smock-wearing, kid working part time at your local department store to make enough money to cover a car insurance bill or music-buying habit. It does not refer to a minimum-wage employee who answers customer questions when not stocking the shelves or mopping the floors. It means the full-time salesperson who sells big-ticket items like cars, boats, or houses. It means the person who is paid only in commission for successful sales, who only eats when customers are buying.

The term "selling," here, means the ability to approach a customer who is "just browsing" and, in a completely friendly manner, create such a desire within that customer for a product that the customer insists on purchasing the product right away. Effective selling is not simply a matter of letting the world know that a product or service is available. As a matter of fact, selling has nothing to do with letting people know about the availability of a product. (That is marketing and will be covered in the next part.) The salesperson's job is about communicating the benefits of one or more available products in such a way that potential customers make their own decision to purchase.

The first task for a salesperson is to assess the needs of the customer and match that customer with the appropriate product. The next thing that must be done is to give a detailed explanation of the benefits of the product for the customer. Throughout the explanation process, the salesperson asks questions to make sure that the customer understands how the product would be beneficial and to make sure the sales process is proceeding as planned. The direction of the presentation can and will change any time the customer shows signs of disinterest. The salesperson's goal is simple: they must tap into customers' emotions and create a desire for the product that is intense enough to make customers choose to purchase.

If the salesperson talks the customer into purchasing a product or uses high-pressure techniques to close the sale, the customer may feel coerced, regret the decision to buy, and possibly even return the product. Since salespeople live on commissions from their sales, it is extremely important that their customers are pleased with their decision to buy. The more they feel that the salesperson is their friend, working with their best interests in mind, the happier they are and the more likely they are to return for future purchases and to refer friends. This means fewer complaints, fewer returns, and more future customers with less effort!

Once customers have made the decision to purchase a product or service, it is the salespersons' task to guide them through the purchase process. They explain all the paperwork, make sure that there are no errors in the information, and explain the customer's options, such as a warranty, service contract, or maintenance plan that protects the customer from faulty merchandise (and also, often, provides the salesperson with the largest commission). All the way through the process, the salesperson is there to help the customer through any difficulties (and ensure the successful completion of the sale).

After the sale is complete, the salesperson will often contact the customer to thank them for the business, to make sure the customer is happy, to reinforce the benefits of the customer's purchase decision, and to ask if they require any further assistance. The follow-up call is made to reinforce the ideas that were instilled in the sales process: that the customer made a good purchase choice and will be happy with the benefits of what was purchased and that the salesperson is a friend who is looking out for the customer's best interests and is willing to help in any way necessary.

Let's look at that process again, in a more concise format:

Form a relationship and develop a rapport with the customers and find out what they need.

Match the customer needs to a product.

Explain the benefits of the product in a manner that creates a desire to purchase.

Lead the customers through the purchase process.

Follow up after the sale.

Does that list look at all familiar? In case the answer is no, here is the same list again. The steps have not been changed, but a few words have been updated to reflect an educational point of view:

Form a relationship and develop a rapport with the students and find out what they know.

Match the student needs to a lesson.

Explain the lesson content in a manner that creates a desire to possess the knowledge.

Lead the students through the learning and practice process.

Follow up (review) after the lesson.

Look familiar now? That's all there is to it. You are in sales. You are selling knowledge and skills to students and their parents. Your job is to get the students (with the parents' support) to make the decision to purchase the knowledge. The process is most effective this way because the students will learn and retain information better if it is *their* idea to make the purchase of knowledge. If they feel forced or coerced, they will be unhappy and will not give their full attention to the learning process.

When students purchase knowledge, they do not pay in cash. Instead, they pay in something that is much more valuable to them at their stage in life: their time and their efforts. It should not surprise you that your students would rather play than do homework, nor that they would rather watch television than strain their brains over a new and difficult concept. With this in mind, you must understand that convincing children to give their time and effort to a new skill is quite similar to convincing adults to part with their cash—only probably more difficult.

It is also important to understand that, although you can accomplish your task if you just sell to the student, your job will be much easier if you sell to the parent as well. Parents will also buy in with time and effort rather than with cash. Parental time and effort could be necessary to help the student understand homework or to get the student to even *do* the homework. It could be spent reinforcing concepts or the benefits of learning while the student is at home. It could be spent doing something to support you or your efforts with the entire class. The bottom line is that selling the parents makes it much easier to sell the students and keep them on track.

Parents can be more difficult to sell than the students. Some will not have to be sold. They will be right with you. These are the parents who participate in the PTO and volunteer to help in your classroom. The parents you have to work to sell are the ones who feel that they have much more important things to do than spend time raising their child. These are the ones who do not attend conferences or even return phone calls. The sale is tough because of the attitude of the parent and because it must be accomplished with minimal personal contact.

Though the selling process and the normal teaching process are very similar in their basic steps, they are very different on one key point. Teaching and selling both include sharing information, but teaching moves straight to this information, whereas selling requires that the salesperson first create an insatiable desire for the product. Thus, when the salesperson is discussing the benefits of the product, the customer pays rapt attention, because it is a subject of intense interest.

If teachers could learn to use this same technique to sell their product (knowledge), they would receive the same benefit of rapt attention and an intense desire to own the product (knowledge). The good news is that teachers can easily learn to do this. What follows is only a brief overview of the process here because the details are the subject of another full book (or even several books).

The key to a successful sales presentation is to focus on the *benefits* of owning the product rather than the product's *features*. A feature is something a product does or a way it works. A benefit is what consumers *get* from the feature. A feature of a television set is a remote control. The benefit is that you can change the channel or the volume without getting up and walking across the room like we had to do in the "old days." For the teacher/salesperson, understanding the difference is paramount.

Customers are after benefits, not features. Customers who ask about features do so because they are looking for the benefits that come from them. A successful salesperson helps to focus the customer's attention on how the benefits of the product in question will make the customer's life better, easier, and more enjoyable. Because all people have an interest in making things better for themselves, the salesperson keeps the focus on "what's in it for me?" When the benefits presented are attractive enough to justify the price in the customer's mind, they will buy.

Students and parents are no different. They want to know what they will get out of learning the information you are teaching. What are the benefits? What will they be able to do that they could not do before? How will this new idea make their lives better, easier, or more enjoyable? How will it help them to get something they want?

Of all the hundreds of tests they must pass in their academic careers, most students study for two tests that they are given in school more than any of the others. Those two tests are the Constitution test and the written test for drivers' education. Time and time again, students who normally do not study at all for a test spend hours, or even *days*, going over the material for these two tests.

The reason for the extra effort is simple. The benefits are clearly stated and universally desired. Students *must* pass the Constitution test to graduate. Students *must* pass the drivers' education test to get their license. In these two cases, the benefits are so greatly desired that no investment of time and effort is too great a price to pay to own the benefit. Students have an *insatiable desire* to possess this knowledge—not because it is of great interest to them but because they have a strong desire for the benefit of possessing the knowledge.

If you can create an equally compelling list of benefits for learning the quadratic equation, the abbreviation for every element on the periodic table, the name and location of every major river in the United States, or *anything* you are teaching, you will get a similar response in the amount of time and effort your students are willing to commit to studying and mastering that information.

Accomplishing this is not easy. As teachers, we learned our subject matter because it was an area of great interest for us or because it was necessary for reaching our goal of becoming teachers. The benefit was that we knew more about a subject we loved or that we were one step closer to our career goal. Unfortunately, we cannot count on our students to be driven by the same desires.

To sell students on learning, teachers must spend time reflecting on the real-world benefits of the lessons being taught. What is the real *benefit* of learning the quadratic equation? What can students do if they learn the elements of the periodic table that they could not do otherwise? How will their lives be easier if they learn the name and location of every U.S. river?

"Because it's in the book" is a good enough reason for many teachers to teach a lesson, but it is not a good enough reason for students to want to learn. Do you want to buy something simply "because it's in the store?" As a teacher/salesperson, you must present compelling reasons (benefits) for your students to *want to* possess the knowledge you are teaching.

14

YOUR RAPPORT CARD

The most difficult customer for a salesperson is the "unmotivated" customer. This is the person who exhibits no strong interest in the product to be sold. These customers are difficult but *not* impossible to sell to. A skillful salesperson faced with this type of customer will find excuses to slow the sales process, such as, "I need to check with my boss about this, but he is in a meeting" or, "Our computer system is running slowly today." They will pass the "extra" time chatting about anything they can think of, but they are not just passing the time. They are working to build rapport with the customer and to come to be thought of as the customer's friend.

There is more to it, though, than just that. They often choose subjects based on the customer's appearance, mannerisms, speech patterns, or something the customer has previously said to them. They are hunting, looking for an opening—a subject or idea of intense interest to the customer—that will help them create a spark of motivation. Once the salesperson finds a subject about which the customer is passionate, they will use that as the starting point for creating a spark within the customer to influence their motivation choices. The salesperson will always make a point to share the passions of the customer, or at least to have an unexplored interest in the subject, so that the conversation can continue in a nonthreatening manner and so that the customer sees the salesperson as a friend rather than an adversary. As the conversation continues, the salesperson will look for ways to tie that subject in with a benefit of the product being sold. The

Figure 14.1. By Cathy Klasek

more positive connections that can be made between subjects important to the customer and the products being sold, the better the chance that the customer will become motivated to buy.

Creating motivation within your students to learn what you are teaching can happen via this same method. Many teachers already know some of the things that are important to their students because of the subjects they choose for projects or essays, their extracurricular activities, or the clothes they wear. More can be learned by starting a "chat" with a student, as a salesperson might, to find a subject of interest to the student that might be suitable as a starting point. It can be as easy as asking what the student did last evening. If the answer is something the student says they do not enjoy, ask what they would rather have been doing.

Once the teacher has found a subject that is important to the unmotivated student, it needs to become a topic of conversation between the student and the teacher. Whenever possible, tie-ins should be made during lessons to connect the subject being studied with the subject important to the student. Make a point to explain why it is important that people interested in _____ (whatever subject is important to the student) understand the concept being taught. As with the sales example above, the more connections a teacher can make between the subjects being taught and the interests or goals of the student, the better the likelihood of the student becoming motivated to buy (learn) the lesson at hand.

Sometimes, the teacher will not be able to make the sale alone. This is common among salespeople, and they have a simple solution: get help! Teachers can generally get the help they need in reaching unmotivated students from many sources if they simply ask for it. Master salespeople look to other salespeople and managers for help in closing a sale. Teachers looking for help in making a sale of knowledge to an unmotivated student can look to a parent, an administrator, a counselor, a social worker, another teacher, or even another student!

Because students are generally taught in groups, teachers can also help unmotivated students to learn using the bell curve principle discussed in chapter 6. Assuming that the teacher has enough control over the positive leaders in the class to keep the followers leaning in a positive direction, the attitudes and pace of the rest of the class can be used as a spark toward motivation. If this is true, the unmotivated student will feel disconnected from the rest of the class and may be looking for ways to be better accepted within the classroom unit.

The teacher can point out that the unmotivated student is preventing his or her classmates from accomplishing a goal or receiving a reward and that the rest of the class would be very happy if the unmotivated student would show some effort. Some students will choose to motivate themselves as a means of better acceptance with the rest of the students. In essence, this is a way to use peer pressure to influence the student's choices in a positive direction.

Before attempting to use this method, the teacher must talk with the positive leaders in the class to make sure that they will comply by accepting and involving the unmotivated student in group work if they change behavior. It is the teacher's job to make sure that the previously unmotivated student receives the attention and acceptance that was promised. A student who changes behaviors to be accepted and sees an increase in acceptance to the group will make the same choice again and again. A student who makes those changes and does *not* see an increase in acceptance will not make the same choice again. Worse, this type of student may become more distant and unmotivated, and will likely lose trust in the teacher.

It is also possible that the unmotivated student is simply not ready to be sold yet. The sales techniques we have been discussing are only really effective with a customer who is at least considering the purchase of the product in question. Before a person becomes a viable prospect to a salesperson, they have to be convinced there is a possibility that they might want to purchase the product in question. This pre-sale work is not done by salespeople; it is done by marketers.

The next part of this book will present a brief overview of some marketing techniques, ways they are used to convince us to do the things we do, and ways they can be used to convince students to do the things we want them to do. Before we get to marketing, let's take a moment to explore some of the methods and techniques used by master salespeople to increase their effectiveness and their likelihood of making a sale. We will also look into how teachers can make use of these same methods and techniques to persuade students and parents to "buy in" to the importance of education.

15

HIGHLY EFFECTIVE HABITS

In order to have success using sales methods to create a desire to learn, you must begin to think like a salesperson. The following is a short list of characteristics common to successful salespeople. Each characteristic is described briefly as to its meaning and its importance in the sales process. Following each description is a short synopsis of the characteristic's value to teachers.

Every available opportunity must be used to build rapport with your customers (both students and parents), to point out the benefits of your product (knowledge), to link benefits of your product with interests of your customers, and to lead your customers down the path from the first sale to the second, the third, and so on. Being constantly on the lookout for opportunities to promote your relationship with your customers (parents and students), to keep them happy, and to promote other products (subjects) for their consideration is a good start on the road to master salesmanship.

Another important quality of a good salesperson is the ability to be constantly enthusiastic and positive. Customers will not buy from negative salespeople or from those who do not seem to be completely behind their product. This can be very difficult because a salesperson's attempts to make a sale are often turned down, but even the worst of days can be turned around by a single customer if the salesperson can leave past failures in the past and continue to move forward with enthusiasm and a positive attitude.

Likewise, a teacher cannot become discouraged by a student who has trouble understanding a new concept or by a class having a hard time making good decisions. These kinds of days can be turned around in an instant by a success. Teachers who allow themselves to become caught up in a bad day will, most likely, miss the opportunity to make this turnaround because of a lack of the positive energy and enthusiasm necessary to affect the change.

Doing this effectively requires further development of your character. The good news for you as a teacher is that, if you have read this far, you have probably already at least begun the process of character development. (If not, now is a good time to start. See part I for details on how to accomplish this.) All you need to do is add a few sales characteristics to the mix. Since constant growth and development are necessary for your character to retain his or her humanity, adding some characteristics of a salesperson to your teacher character can just become a part of the growth process.

Salespeople must always bear in mind that making sales takes time. There is no "silver bullet" that will hurry the process along. Relationships must be built, customer needs must be explored, products and their benefits must be explained, questions must be answered, and paperwork must be completed. Customers do not like to be rushed or pressured. They want to feel that their every concern is valid and that nothing is of greater concern to the salesperson than their complete satisfaction. Attempting to rush the process at any point can result in the customer feeling pressured and can cause the loss of the sale.

Only when all the questions are answered, when the customer is completely satisfied with the decision to purchase, and when the salesperson is viewed as a trusted advisor who is working for the benefit of the customer can the sale be completed. The salesperson must show complete patience as well as confidence in both the product and the customer throughout the entire process. A character can help make this happen.

This is another direct parallel to the role of a teacher. For students to feel comfortable enough to take the chances necessary for learning to take place, a relationship *must* be formed between the teacher and the student. The teacher must be trusted and seen by the student as caring and helpful before any real learning can take place. There is no shortcut here. Time must be spent to build the relationship.

Teachers must show ultimate patience in the face of student problems, inability to grasp new concepts, and repeated poor behavior choices. They must also show complete, unwavering confidence in the ability of every student to rise to the challenges set before them. Both of these tasks become monumentally easier with the development of your superteacher character.

No salesperson is an island. When the sales process stalls, the master salesperson will call for help. Another salesperson or a manager (who is also a salesperson) will be brought in to talk with the customer. Sometimes the original salesperson will leave during this process so that the helper can determine if the cause of the problem is a personal conflict of some sort between the customer and the salesperson. Sometimes both salespeople stay with the customer and perform a "double team" to try to get the sales process moving again.

The bottom line on this point is that no salesperson, no matter how talented, can reach every customer working solo. The master sales professional knows when to call for backup, how to double-team when necessary, and how to work one salesperson against another when necessary to close the sale.

As mentioned before, teachers also need to know where and when to look for help in getting through to difficult students. The best place to look for help will vary from school to school depending on the services available. The best time in the educational process to look for help can only be determined through a thorough knowledge of the student and experience on the part of the teacher.

The last characteristic of a master salesperson to be mentioned here is appearance. A salesperson's appearance is of utmost importance. He or she must be clean and clean-cut in appearance. Hair must be combed, nails trimmed, and clothing professional and adequately pressed. Every detail of the salesperson's appearance must present a picture of professionalism. No detail can detract the customer's attention or focus from the product. No detail can give any hint of anything short of complete professionalism, confidence, success, and pride in the company and the product being represented.

Teachers must (pardon the pun) follow suit. Although we try to teach our students not to judge a person based on how they look, we all do this anyway. Without any background information, a vast majority of people will want to speak with the salesperson who is the best dressed. This person is obviously more knowledgeable, more professional, and higher up the organizational chain of the company to be dressed that way. It is a natural assumption. More educated, more successful, and more important people tend to be better dressed.

This is an area where many teachers drop the ball. They like to try to hold themselves to a double standard where appearance is concerned. They complain that they are not treated with the respect due someone of their high educational stature and that they are not paid at a level commensurate with their level of education and the demands of the job (both perfectly

Figure 15.1. By Cathy Klasek

valid arguments). The double standard comes in when the teachers decide that they should be able to wear jeans and T-shirts to work any time they want. This simply does not fit the picture of a successful and well-educated professional. Yes, there are times when educators need to alter their dress because of classroom activities, spirit weeks, and the like, but this can almost always be done without resorting to jeans and T-shirts. Clothes can be found that look professional but are still comfortable and durable enough for any classroom activity. To do anything less is to try to have your cake and eat it, too. If you want to be thought of, treated, and paid as the professional you are, you must start by dressing the part. Your appearance reflects your opinion of yourself and of the level and importance of your work. Why should anyone treat you as a highly trained professional when your appearance shows that *you* don't think it is true?

In many school districts, wearing jeans to work is allowed and is a regular occurrence for teachers. This is a bad idea. When teachers wear jeans to school, the line between teacher and student becomes blurred. If you pay close attention, you will notice that your students are better behaved when you are better dressed. Students see you as less of an authority figure when you are not dressed up, and you behave differently as well. Dressing up should simply be a part of every teacher character.

Some teachers who wear jeans to work try to justify the action with excuses. They may say that they wear jeans to fit in with other faculty members who dress that way. If this is true, it is high time that someone on the faculty began setting a better example. No teacher would accept the excuse that an A student was getting C grades in order to win friends in the class. If the teachers in your building give you grief about dressing professionally when they don't, encourage them to rise to your level of professionalism. If they refuse to at least accept your desire to be seen as a professional, it may be time to get new friends.

Other teachers will say that they wear jeans so that they can "fit in" better with the students and so that the students could see that they are "just a regular person." This is a bad idea. It sends a mixed message to the students. You are *not* a "regular person." You are "superteacher," and you have to stay that way to remain effective. As soon as you become a "regular person" in the eyes of the students, there is no reason for them to listen to you or follow your rules. You are not someone to be respected and listened to; you are "just a regular person."

Every occupation that carries authority over or responsibility for others comes with a uniform of some sort. Members of the military, police, fire and rescue, doctors, and nurses all have a uniform that indicates (is a symbol of) their position and responsibility. Because it indicates their responsibility, the uniform also commands respect. That respect is necessary to the successful completion of the tasks assigned to those professionals. Without their uniforms, it would be more difficult for any of these professionals to do their jobs.

The teacher's uniform is professional business attire—as much as is possible and practical given the subject being taught and the activities of the day. Teachers send a mixed message to students when they dress like a "regular person" and then try to command the respect of their students. The mixed message causes confusion and detracts from the lesson. The same mixed message is sent to parents, community, administrators, and school board members when the teachers dress like "regular people" (jeans and T-shirts) and then ask to be treated and paid as trained and experienced professionals. Jeans do not fit the "superteacher" character. If you like to wear jeans, go ahead . . . just not when you are teaching.

Teachers are salespeople selling the benefits of knowledge to students and parents. To successfully make the sale, the salesperson must completely look and feel the part of the professional at all times; and, unless you are selling seed corn, that look does *not* include denim.

MORE INFORMATION ON SALES TECHNIQUES

The different ways teachers can use sales techniques to improve student attention and retention could fill several books. Teachers who can use these techniques to convince their students to "buy in" to the lessons being presented will experience incredible educational success. Though books detailing these techniques for educational purposes do not currently exist, help is still available.

If you are interested in learning some of the techniques of sales professionals so that you can improve your effectiveness as an educator, the answers are as close as your nearest library. There are thousands of books available on effective selling and sales techniques. Check out one or more of these books. All you have to do to turn a book on sales techniques into a book on education and motivation techniques is replace each occurrence of the word "product" with the word "lesson," "concept," or "knowledge," and replace each occurrence of the word "customer," or "client" with the word "student." Try it!

IV

MARKETING

16

BECOMING THE PIED PIPER

Though they may seem like the same subject, marketing and sales are actually quite different from one another, both in approach and in goals. Sales, as outlined in part III, involves a process of learning the needs of specific customers, matching those needs to products, explaining the benefits of the matching products and how they connect to the customer needs, and providing support for the customer through and following the sales process. A salesperson's job shares many of the same responsibilities as a teacher's job.

Marketing, however, is a different animal. Marketing is generally aimed at groups, not individuals. Marketing creates initial interest in a product among a general population. Marketing creates the desire to own a product. Marketing gets a customer to get off the couch and go talk to the salesperson in the first place. To borrow and expand upon an old cliché, getting an Eskimo to buy ice takes a great salesman; getting the Eskimo to drive his dogsled fifty miles for the *opportunity* to buy ice takes great marketing. Because marketing creates the initial desire to do, buy, or learn something, it is also an essential tool in the teacher's toolbox.

The amount of marketing we are all exposed to on a daily basis is staggering. While the different applications of marketing techniques are almost limitless, as evidenced in the wide variety of advertisements we see daily, the basic principles and techniques of marketing are relatively few. Nearly all advertising can be boiled down to applications of one or more of these few powerful principles and techniques.

Figure 16.1. By Cathy Klasek

Robert Cialdini, a recognized and highly respected authority on this topic, refers to the principles of marketing as "weapons of influence" because they are the tools, or weapons, used daily by professional marketers to influence the behavior patterns and buying habits of consumers everywhere. All are powerful psychological principles, and all are used because they consistently work.

The teacher who understands these principles and learns to apply them in the classroom can become a master of the art of marketing and influence. Since teachers are expected to teach behavior, self-discipline, personal habits, and a lifelong love of learning in addition to their "official" subject matter, a basic knowledge of the most effective methods (weapons) of influencing the behavior of others is most useful.

As you begin the study of marketing techniques for the purpose of incorporating them into your classroom, it is likely you will find that some of the methods of persuasion you are currently using in your classes are based on one or more of these methods. Most successful teachers will recognize one or more of the things they do in their classes within the following descriptions.

Learning about the marketing concepts and the psychological principles behind them will allow you to analyze *why* the things you are already doing in class are working or not working. It will allow you to revise your methods and procedures to make them even more effective. It all starts by developing an understanding of the following marketing (psychological) principles.

In the following pages, each psychological or marketing principle (weapon of influence) will be presented in its most basic form along with a brief example or two of how it is used for marketing purposes. As these principles are introduced, you may notice some parallels to ideas covered in the section on sales. Sales and marketing are different disciplines, but there is some overlap. To be effective, salespeople must have customers to work with. They will use principles of marketing to get customers to choose to work with them rather than with another salesperson. In other words, salespeople market themselves so that they have the opportunity to sell their products.

Following the introduction of each principle will be a few ideas for how the idea can be incorporated into a classroom. These sections are intentionally short. The specific applications of each principle are limited only by your imagination. The goal of these sections is not to give you a turnkey solution but simply to give you a starting point and to spark your imagination. Once you understand the principles, you can use them to design your own applications that fit your classroom, your students, and your teacher character.

Following the list of possible educational applications will be a short section labeled "The Caveat." All marketing principles have one of these. Under certain conditions and circumstances, each principle becomes less effective or completely ineffective. These are things to watch out for as you experiment with the application of these ideas into your classroom.

RESEARCH AND DEVELOPMENT

There is one important point to keep in mind as you begin to learn about marketing and develop ideas for use in your classroom: while there is a definite science to the ways in which we can be influenced, the successful individual application of the principles has no science. It is completely art. Professional marketers are all intimately familiar with the principles outlined here, but they still have to guess at the effectiveness of any certain application or wording. When designing a campaign, marketers will sketch out several ideas—some only removed from one another by a word or two—and test them out on a small sample audience. Data from the tests is gathered to determine which idea has produced the best results. These ideas are then analyzed, modified, and tested again to find out if their effectiveness can be improved. This process of research and development in the application of marketing ideas is an essential part of the process of designing a marketing campaign. The only way to find out which exact wording, graphic, layout, and so forth, will be most effective in an advertisement is to test it out, track the results, and make comparisons.

The same will be true of your classroom. There are no absolutes in marketing or in classrooms. Application of these principles will increase your success in achieving your goals with your students, but the only way to reach maximum effect is through trial and error. Invent an application, test it, track the results, change the application slightly, test it, track the results, change the application slightly again, test it, . . .

17

WEAPONS OF MASS INSTRUCTION

RECIPROCATION

The Marketing Principle

"Thanks, I owe you one."

This simple and common statement is the basis behind a powerful psychological principle and marketing technique. When someone does something for us, we feel obligated to return the favor. For most people, the idea of being indebted to someone else is very uncomfortable.

Archaeologists and anthropologists have found evidence of this system of trading favors in every human culture since the beginning of time. It is a part of every society on the face of the earth. It is believed to be a building block of human social evolution. It allows individuals to specialize in different areas of expertise without worry about receiving all they need to survive from specialists in other areas within the group. It was, and still is, a huge benefit to society as a whole and is deeply ingrained in all of us.

We have all learned to obey the reciprocation rule. We also know that those who fail to obey the rule are looked down upon and treated harshly by the rest of society. When someone does a favor for us, whether we asked the person to or not, we feel a need to return that favor. The need to return the favor hangs over our heads, and the feeling of obligation consumes us until we find a way to do a favor in return. The need to be free of this indebtedness is so strong that we are willing to go to extraordinary lengths to "even the score." In other words, the person who owes the favor is willing to do a much larger favor in return, just to be free of the debt.

We have all experienced this marketing technique. The salespeople at many car dealerships offer a drink to anyone who walks in the door. Donation solicitations in the mail often include "free gifts" such as personalized return address labels. The Hare Krishna faithful always give away a free flower before asking for a donation. The list goes on and on. The technique is used constantly for one simple reason: it works.

The Educational Tie-in

Doing small favors for students can cause them to feel obligated to return favors to you. Picking up a dropped pencil, giving a student a little extra time to finish a test, spending a little extra time after school or during lunch to help a student better understand a lesson, or bringing in cookies or some other treat can be viewed as a favor and cause the student to feel indebted to you.

The favors can be returned through almost anything if the request is phrased properly. Including "Would you do me a favor?"; "It would really help me if . . ."; or "I would really appreciate it if . . ." in your requests for student work or behaviors frames the actions as favors that the students can do for you in order to even the score, or "erase their debt."

The Caveat

The principle of reciprocation becomes completely ineffective when customers (students) start to believe that you are only doing favors for them so that you can get something in return. At this point, the favor ceases to be a favor. Instead, it is viewed as a controlling device. Be careful to avoid creating a cause-and-effect relationship in your students' minds when using this weapon.

Avoid statements like "I did _____ for you, so now you have to _____ for me." The strength of the reciprocation rule may get you the desired result once with this approach, but future favors you do for your students will be viewed as attempts at control rather than genuine favors, and future attempts to have the favors reciprocated will likely end in failure.

AUTHORITY

The Marketing Principle

As a society, we are conditioned to respond to symbols of authority. When we are given instructions to do something by a person in a position of authority, we comply. Compliance to authority figures is important to the working of our society. Authority figures make and enforce rules to keep us safe. Medical professionals tell us what to do to keep us healthy. Police officers tell us what to do to be safe and stay out of trouble. Bosses tell us what to do to keep our jobs. Parents tell children what to do to become responsible adults. And the list goes on and on.

These are all beneficial reasons to do what we are told by authority figures. No one would ever use that type of blind obedience against us, right? Wrong. Marketers use authority figures and "experts" all the time to influence our thinking. "Doctor recommended"; "the brand dentists use"; and "I'm not just the president, I'm also a member" are just a few of the many lines used in advertising to let us know that an expert is telling us what to do.

The interesting thing about this principle from a psychological standpoint is that people are so conditioned to do what the "experts" tell us that we will almost always follow instructions without bothering to find out if the "expert" giving the instructions is an *actual* expert. We are so conditioned to believe experts that the mere appearance of expertise is enough to gain compliance in most instances. The doctors and dentists in most television commercials are not real doctors and dentists. Actors, by dressing the part and speaking with an air of authority, convince audiences that they are genuine experts, and people are often ready to follow the advice given without further thought.

On a smaller scale, salespeople who give us tips about the quality, or lack of quality, of one item versus another tend to be viewed as experts by the customers they help. These salespeople can then use their expert status, the trust it gains them, and the reciprocation principle to convince customers to spend more than they had originally planned.

The Educational Tie-in

Parents and students are taught to listen to experts and authority figures and obey their instructions. Since one of the main objectives of educators in general is to get our students to listen and do as they are told, this principle should be tailor-made for teachers. While the principle can and should be used, it can easily fall prey to caveats that must be examined first.

The Caveat

Students know that they are to obey authority figures and that teachers are authority figures. However, they also like to test the limits of their own individuality and authority. Because the students know that most teacher instructions do not have anything to do with their personal health or safety, the classroom is a place where they will test the limits of their ability to defy authority. The teacher, therefore, must constantly guard the line of authority that must not be crossed through the consistent use of discipline.

Students and parents expect that school, like home, will be a place where students are disciplined for mistakes but are still loved and helped in spite of their errors. Depending on a student's situation at home, school may be the safest place for these tests of individuality and power. Teachers must be prepared to have their authority tested more than the authority principle would generally suggest.

Another problem with the use of this principle in the field of education is that the teacher, simply by virtue of always being present, may not be viewed as "special" enough to be an expert. This is simply a result of familiarity and is in no way related to a teacher's actual knowledge or ability. If you have run into this problem in the past, take heart. The Bible tells us that even Jesus had to deal with this. In his hometown of Nazareth, the people did not listen to His teachings. They became caught up in the idea that they had known Him since childhood. Since the villagers knew that Jesus had not undergone specialized training to learn the things He was teaching, they naturally assumed that He could not possibly know what He was talking about. The villagers, who had known Jesus as a young boy and seen him grow up, could not imagine that He had become anything more than the young boy they once knew.

There is an old, somewhat tongue-in-cheek, adage that an expert is defined as "someone from out of town." Though the tone of the definition is clearly facetious, there is an underlying truth. Authority figures, like teachers, are held up on a pedestal and thought of as characters more than as actual humans. When people find out that the authority figure is known to be just a normal person like you or me, some of the reverence for authority and expertise is lost.

A balance must be struck between the expertise and authority afforded by the title "teacher" and the loss of those qualities as a result of familiarity. A consistently applied superteacher character (with a matching consistently professional appearance) can help a teacher keep that balance in place.

The Educational Tie-in

One way to keep the scales of the authority principle tipped in the teacher's favor is to understand how authority is created by marketing and sales professionals. One important element is appearance. To be accepted without question, an expert must *look* the part. Police, firefighters, and medical professionals all have uniforms that let us know they are symbols of authority in their fields. If these same people give members of the public the same instructions when they are out of uniform, it is much more likely that they will not be accepted as experts and will, therefore, be ignored. Likewise, teachers should consistently wear their "uniform" of business attire to maintain their appearance of expertise.

Confidence is another important element in the use of the authority principle. Authority figures are expected to be confident in their expertise. Posture, composure, and tone of voice must all contribute to the appearance of expertise. In teacher terms, this means that lessons must be well prepared and that the teacher character must maintain confidence and composure at all times.

Providing "inside information" is a powerful tool used by marketers to establish authority. Adding "secret" tips and tricks to the presentation of lessons will not only create the appearance of authority and expertise on a subject but also greatly increase student attention. Everyone likes to know the "secrets" of a subject or the "easier" way to remember something or to accomplish a task.

Guest speakers are another great way to make use of the authority principle. Because guest speakers are chosen by the teacher and invited into the classroom to speak about a subject, they will automatically be viewed by the students as an expert. The students are more likely to heed advice from the guest than from you, because of this heightened expert status. To be brought in as a guest to speak to the class, this person must know even *more* than the superteacher. If the guest expert reinforces things the teacher has already said, those points will become more powerful still.

While guest speakers do need to be thoroughly knowledgeable on a subject to be a benefit to your students, they do not necessarily have to be world-renowned authorities. Anyone who can speak intelligently on his or her subject, who looks and acts the part, and who has been invited by the teacher will be accepted as an expert.

SCARCITY

The Marketing Principle

Every collector knows that rare items become more valuable simply as a result of their rarity. This is simple supply-and-demand economics. The economic principle, though, is based on a deeper psychological principle that causes us to desire items that are in short supply or are difficult to obtain more than those that are readily available. Marketers use this knowledge to create a desire for products by creating scarcity. "For a limited time only"; "enrollment is limited"; "these will never be available again"; "last chance"; "only six are left"; "limit two per customer"; and "three days only" are examples of phrases commonly used by marketers applying the scarcity principle.

Study of the principle has shown that it is much more persuasive to advertise things consumers might *lose* if they *fail* to do something than it is to advertise things that consumers will *gain* if they *succeed* in doing something. This same idea is behind the saying "a bird in the hand is worth two in the bush." People tend to work harder to hold on to the things they have than they are willing to work to gain something new.

Another use of the scarcity principle is in what social scientists call "psychological reactance." Simply put, this is the natural tendency to want the things we are told we cannot have. With this in mind, marketers create "insurmountable" barriers to the acquisition of something in order to cause consumers to want it so much that they work to discover the "loophole" that allows them to possess the item.

Nothing can generate more psychological reactance than the loss (or *apparent* loss) of an established freedom. Such was the case with prohibition in the 1920s. The law was passed in an attempt to stop the use of alcohol, but because people considered this to be a loss of an established freedom, the result was increased alcohol use and the advancement of organized crime in order to provide alcohol to consumers who now wanted it more than ever. The law's existence actually created *more* demand for alcohol than had previously existed.

The Educational Tie-in

The scarcity principle is quite powerful and useful in educational settings. It can be a powerful motivational tool to encourage your top students to push themselves to perform at their best. Incentives and rewards for the first three students to finish an assignment or the top five grades on a test are very effective applications of the principle. The type of reward and the number available should be tailored to fit your students and your goals for the application. If you are designing an incentive to challenge your brightest students to do even better, the number of awards available should be less than the number of bright students you think would be interested in winning so that the award is sufficiently scarce. If you are trying to motivate an entire class, try using a "limited time only" type of application. An example of this type of application would be a benefit or reward offered to anyone who completes an assignment and turns it in before the due date. This gives all students a chance to gain the reward if they are willing to do their work early.

The scarcity principle can be used with the idea of avoiding a loss as well. Informing students that they will lose the opportunity to do something if they fail to complete a task or accomplish a goal is an example. This is the psychological principle that gets students to study so hard for their written driving exam. They have been told that if they do not pass the test, they will lose the ability to earn their driver's licenses. The motivation created is strong.

Psychological reactance is also an important and powerful motivational tool for educators to understand. The same psychological phenomenon that causes students to rebel against teacher authority can be used against students to get them to willingly give their best efforts to a project at the teacher's direction.

For example, at the conclusion of the presentation of a lesson, the teacher could put a question or problem on the board concerning the new material. As the question is going onto the board, the teacher could announce that no one will be able to answer the question because it is too difficult and could only be answered by a student who was *really* paying attention during the lesson. For the students to understand how to answer the question, the teacher will *certainly* have to go through the explanation step by step because no student has *ever* answered this question without help. The teacher's announcement about the difficulty of the question is a *challenge* to the students. Psychological reactance kicks in, and the students will work as hard as they can to answer the question to show the teacher that he or she is wrong about the extent of their abilities. The beauty of the principle is that it is so engrained in the students' psychological makeup to test their own limits that they will not bother to think about what they are doing. They will simply react and work to prove you wrong. The more you insist that they cannot do something, the more they will work to accomplish just what you said they couldn't do.

The Caveat

Scarcity is a powerful marketing and educational tool that is effective because it is difficult to resist. As with all educational tools, however, if this principle is applied too often in the exact same manner, students will begin to become accustomed to it and the effect will be lessened. Variation is a key to the continued effectiveness of the scarcity principle. If each application of the principle looks a little different than the last, the result of its use will continue to be positive. For ideas on how to apply the principle in class, look to your mailbox, newsstand, e-mail account, and television. Solicitation letters, magazine and newspaper ads, e-mail ads, and television commercials use the principle constantly in attempts to control consumer behavior. The variations are many, but the underlying principle is the same for one simple reason: it works.

Another potential caveat of the classroom use of the scarcity principle is lack of motivation in students with lower abilities. If the rewards are always given to the top students, those students who struggle in class will lose motivation because they will feel they can never win. Again, variation is the key to the continued effectiveness of the technique. Make sure that incentives are offered to all students. Consider ideas such as a scarcity principle reward for the students whose score on an assignment increases the most over their previous test grade or current class grade. With some thought and creativity, the scarcity principle can be applied in different ways to provide motivational opportunities to all of your students.

COMMITMENT AND CONSISTENCY

The Marketing Principle

"Because I said so, that's why!"

Who would have thought that this standard Mom and Dad answer would turn out to be rooted in an incredibly strong psychological and marketing principle? Consistency is a highly valued trait. It is expected of all of us and we know it. When a friend tells us they are going to do something for us, we expect them to follow through and do it. We get upset when people do not live up to their word. Likewise, we do not want to be seen as a person who does not live up to their word. As a matter of fact, we will go to nearly absurd lengths to keep from going back on our word.

Any time psychologists find a principle that will cause this type of motivation, marketers are certain to find a way to exploit it. The marketing application is extremely straightforward. It is often used in combination with the idea that human nature causes us to brag a bit, to claim a bit more than is actually true, in order to impress others. Once these types of statements (commitments) have been made, the marketer backs us into a corner to live up to our word (consistency). At this point, we must either admit to bragging (lying) or follow through on our statement by agreeing to the marketer's request. A marketer will ask you questions about your activities, your beliefs, or your plans. Based on your answer, you may be asked to purchase a product that would be perfect for a person with your beliefs and activities, to do something to support your stated beliefs, or to do some extra work that aligns with your stated plans.

Another application of this principle is used to draw people in to support a cause or activity a step at a time. In this application, the customer is asked to do something small, simple, and seemingly harmless to help out. If a customer agrees to do this, they are contacted a couple of weeks later, thanked for their support, and asked to do something slightly larger to show their continued support. The further the pattern continues, the more the customer feels compelled to comply with every request to avoid contradicting what they have already done.

The Educational Tie-in

Teachers actually use this principle all the time. They will guide a student to a small success in a subject and then tell them that since they were able to complete the newly finished task, they are certainly able to complete another (usually larger and longer) task on their own.

Teachers are using this idea when they use behavior contracts. Once the plan for behavior change is on paper and agreed to by the student, the student is likely to feel bound to follow through on the commitment they made and do their best to change. These contracts usually start by working on changing something small to ensure the student has success and then moving on to larger and more difficult behaviors. Once the student has accomplished the first goal, he or she is more likely to agree to work on a second, larger goal to appear consistent with what they have done in the past.

The principle, though commonly used, is *not* commonly understood. Knowing the psychology behind the ideas can help teachers not only to expand their use of this psychological principle but also to increase their effectiveness with each application.

The Caveats

There are two potential caveats here. For this psychological principle to be effective, it must be applied properly. The customer (student) cannot have a good reason to refuse the first request and cannot know that there will be a similar, larger request coming in the future. The second request should not follow the first too closely to avoid giving the student the feeling of being set up. This is not a principle to be used on a whim. The sequence of events and timing should be planned out before you begin.

The other potential pitfall of this technique is that it will not always work with all students. Some will respond well to this type of plan, but some students are, by their very nature, or by nature of their age or stage of development, inconsistent. One of the goals of schools is to teach our students the consistency that will be expected of them by society. Depending of the level of development of the student you are working with, this method may be invalid.

LIKING

The Marketing Principle

The liking principle is simple: we are more likely to buy more products if we are asked by someone we know and like. The ways that marketers, who do not even know you, use this principle border on the downright devious.

Applications of the liking principle can be as simple and straightforward as a product party. This concept was pioneered by Tupperware but has been used by many other companies as well: A host invites friends to a party, where a product line is displayed and demonstrated. Before the end of the party, all the guests are asked to make a purchase to benefit their friend, the host. (This also applies the reciprocation principle: guests buy products as a way of returning a favor to the host, who was kind enough to invite them to the party.) This business model is so effective that Tupperware is no longer available at commercial outlets. It can only be found at a Tupperware party. The only way to get Tupperware now is to attend, or host, a party. (They are applying the scarcity principle, too—these guys are *good*.)

While the Tupperware approach is a fairly obvious application of the liking principle, there are many others that are far less obvious. Research has shown that we tend to like people who are similar to us in opinions, personality, backgrounds, or any one of many other traits. Marketers, then, will try to make sure that the people in their ads dress, speak, and act like their potential customers. Salespeople will use this principle as well. Besides attempting to be interested in the same subjects, as was discussed earlier, salespeople will mirror potential clients in posture, gesture, mood, and verbal style. Customers unconsciously notice the similarities and, as a result, like the salespeople more.

Marketers and salespeople will also go out of their way to compliment their customers. We like people who like us. Compliments are signs that marketers and salespeople like us and appreciate things about us. We automatically like them in return. How could someone who thinks we are awesome be bad?

Association can also create liking. Marketers work to associate their products with something we already have positive feelings about (something or someone we already like). This is the reason for celebrity product endorsements. It is also why so many sales pitches follow free food and why so many ads for cars, beds, and so forth include pictures of attractive models.

The Educational Tie-in

The educational uses of this principle are as unlimited as the marketing applications. The bottom line is simple. If the students like you or the subject, they are more likely to comply with your requests. If they like you *and* the subject, the chances for compliance are even higher.

To put the liking principle to work for you at school, simply follow the lead of marketing professionals. The Tupperware party can become a special, invitation-only party in your classroom over lunch. Invite students to the party. (Make sure they are friends.) During the course of the lunch or party, play some simple games that have to do with the subject you want to teach, and have some prizes. Allow some time for the students to just talk and enjoy each other's company. This approach takes advantage of association to connect a subject with a party and some special time with the teacher.

This idea can be tied in with the scarcity principle as well. An invitation to the party can be earned by only those students who earn a certain grade, read a certain number of books, go a certain amount of time without a classroom discipline problem, or whatever other goal you create for them. Scarcity is the motivation, and liking is the reward—a classroom marketing win-win.

Talk with your students informally. When possible, mirror their interests, postures, and styles. Of course, this cannot be done all the time. You still need to hold the line between teacher and student. Continue to dress like a teacher. Maintain your superteacher character. Do not mirror attitudes that are negative toward school or other people. It is not necessary to mirror every detail for the principle to be effective. One or two traits will do.

Look for reasons to compliment your students and take advantage of the opportunities. Compliments let your students know that you like them. In return, they will like you, too. Make certain that compliments are genuine and heartfelt. Students will easily pick up on false praise and like you less because of it.

Associate a subject that your students do not like with games, incentives, and other things that they *do* like. This idea will work best if the game or incentive is associated only with one subject. When the only way to get to play a really fun game is to work on a not-so-fun subject, the wanted association will be made.

The liking principle is one of the best marketing principles to apply to education. Students who like a teacher or subject are not only more likely to comply with a request but also more likely to pay attention, more likely to retain information, and less likely to be disruptive. If students are studying a subject they like with a teacher they also like, then having them in your class is a joy.

HUMOR

The Marketing Principle

The use of humor is also employed by marketers and salespeople to create liking. Someone who makes you laugh is at the same time likeable and memorable. This is why so many television advertisements are built around humor. It makes the product memorable and creates an association in the consumer's mind between laughter and the product. The result? Instant liking (and increased sales).

The Educational Tie-in

Teachers should use this idea liberally. If you can make your students laugh on a regular basis, they will not just like you—they will *love* you! The humor you employ during lessons can be related to the lesson, but it doesn't have to be. Random knock-knock jokes, silly voices, callbacks, or running gags will help keep them listening and get them to like you. This liking will translate into students who are willing to comply with nearly any request you make of them.

The Caveat

The real danger in the application of this principle in a school setting is taking things too far and trying to become your students' buddy. A teacher must remain a teacher (or, better yet, a superteacher) at all times. A teacher can be friendly toward students without worry, but once a teacher becomes a friend, the respect necessary for classroom discipline begins to erode. When this happens, the teacher—friend to the student or not—becomes less liked.

Students expect teachers to maintain discipline in the classroom. A teacher who consistently and fairly disciplines students will be liked for this even (and sometimes especially) by the students who are disciplined the most.

The association method within this principle must be applied carefully because it works in both directions. If the students associate a subject with something they enjoy, their liking for the subject will increase. On the other hand, if the students associate a subject with a negative experience, they will *dislike* the subject even more.

Within appropriate subject matter, there is no caveat to the use of humor to increase liking and to entertain (hold attention) during lessons. Make sure, though, that you leave enough time for the students to react to the humor. Stepping on a laugh can confuse your students and make them afraid to react to anything in class.

18

LIKING, ASSOCIATION, AND DOG TRAINING

Association is an application of the liking principle wherein marketers try to create an association between two otherwise unconnected objects. If this seems to you to be reminiscent of Pavlov, you are correct. Pavlov proved the reflexive nature of this principle with his famous experiments. By ringing a bell every time he offered food to his dogs, he caused the dogs to associate the bell with food. Soon they would salivate (their normal reaction to being fed) when the bell was rung but no food was offered.

The experiments merely proved the psychological principle to be true. The dogs, bell-ringing, and salivating are not necessary parts of the principle. Exactly the same process is taking place when we associate Michael Jordan with Hanes undergarments. The principle is universal. To prove the point, allow me to relate a story from my first year as a teacher. (This one is *not* made up!)

> My first teaching job was far away from anyone I knew, so when a colleague announced that she was looking for a home for a puppy, I volunteered. I had never had a dog before, so I bought a book on how to care for and train dogs. The book was quite detailed and useful. As I read it, some points jumped out as important:
>
> - Dogs do not understand the words you say, but they understand the tone of voice you use quite well.
> - Don't stay mad at the dog for long. It doesn't have the attention span to remember why you are upset.

Figure 18.1. By Cathy Klasek

LIKING, ASSOCIATION, AND DOG TRAINING

- If the dog does something wrong (tears something up, goes potty in the house, etc.), and you are not there to see it happen, you need to rub the dog's nose in the offending area as you discipline it or it will not associate the discipline with the behavior.
- When beginning to train the dog, give the command (e.g., sit), force it to comply (e.g., push its bottom down on the floor), and then praise the dog for doing it correctly and give it a treat.
- Training and discipline must be frequent and completely consistent for the dog to learn and to not become confused.
- Dogs are pack animals. They need to feel that they are a part of a group (pack). Packs can include humans.
- Every pack needs to have a leader, an alpha dog. If a human does not establish him- or herself as the pack leader, the dog will assume the role and will be virtually untrainable.
- Dogs need attention, love, and play to be happy, healthy, and responsive. Dogs who do not receive the attention they need will act out.

Now it may just have been me and the fact that, as a first-year teacher, I was having difficulty with my junior high students, but this struck me as a perfect match for junior high. My principal had told me that to have better success with junior high students I needed to understand the "animal" (*his* word, not mine) better. Here was a book on training animals, and it sounded like a reasonable match to me. So I tried it. And it worked!

- Most junior high students are much more concerned with the new, incredible rush of hormones running through their bodies and changing them into their adult forms than they are with anything their teachers have to say. Even though they know the language, they do *not* listen to all the words. They *do*, however, listen to the tone of voice used.
- They do not remember past actions for very long and will get confused if you stay mad at them for a long time or if you try to discipline them for something without explaining *exactly* what it is that they did wrong.
- One of the best ways to teach them a new skill is to explain it, drag them through it step by step, and then praise them for doing so well.
- Lessons must be reviewed consistently or they will be forgotten. Inconsistent classroom expectations or applications of discipline will result in student confusion. Student confusion about the types of behavior acceptable in class will lead to poor behavior choices.
- One of the goals of every junior high student is to fit in, to be a part of groups. One such group is a classroom. Every classroom needs a leader (alpha dog). If the teacher does not establish him- or herself as that leader, a student will take over the role and the class will become virtually uncontrollable.
- Students who do not receive the attention, affection, and fun that they crave will act out until they receive it or will attempt to create it for themselves.

It seemed to me to be an absolutely perfect match, so I applied the methods outlined in the book both at home and at school and found that both the dog and the junior high students got better at doing what I wanted them to do.

Though I had not yet made the connection to marketing methods, this was the event that made me begin to understand that sometimes some of the best teaching methods can come from places other than educational texts and college textbooks.

These same techniques apply equally well to students of all ages. There are some minor differences in the way they must be implemented in the classroom, but the basic tenets apply to everyone—even adults. Perhaps that is why people and dogs get along so well—we are all looking for the same things.

MORE INFORMATION

As with the section on sales techniques, there are literally thousands of books available on principles and techniques of marketing. If you would like to learn more about how marketers convince us to do the things they want us to do, the answers are as close as your nearest library or bookstore.

These books were not written with educators in mind, so they will not include classroom applications of the concepts. However, because these books contain explanations of the methods marketers use to convince us to do what they want, it is fairly easy to read these books with the eyes of a teacher and imagine ways that you might apply the techniques in classroom situations.

Remember that the only way to find out which applications of these techniques will work for you and how to apply them for the best classroom results is to experiment. Try out new ideas and then try variations until you arrive at what works best for your students, your teacher character, and your situation.

V

LOOSE ENDS

19

TYING UP LOOSE ENDS

As you read through the ideas presented so far, you have probably recognized some things that you are already doing. If you have already discovered some of these ideas intuitively, that's great. Most teachers who do these sorts of things in class do them "because they work." These teachers, now armed with the *reasons* their techniques work, can become even *more* effective.

The following are some odds and ends that, though they did not fit into the previous chapters, are extremely important. They represent the basis of everything that has been presented. They are guidelines for everything presented this far. The book would not be complete without their inclusion.

FIVE AND FORTY-FIVE

All educators should understand the significance of the above two numbers. Failing to understand them can result in widespread student "boredom" and a catastrophic failure in the educational process.

Five Minutes

Research has determined that the average length of a human attention span is only about five minutes. (That is down from twelve minutes in 2002.) Most teachers who hear this statistic complain about the evils of television and the Internet and move on to another subject. While it would be nice if our students had longer attention spans, many teachers miss the significance of the idea. Students who are not paying attention cannot be taught. A five-minute attention span means that teaching must be accomplished in short bursts linked together with changes of pace and asides to retain or regain attention.

This is another reason to use the winding-path lessons introduced in chapter 9. Each twist, surprise, story, aside or other such device allows you to restart the five-minute attention clock. By using these techniques, you can extend a lesson well beyond the normal student attention span.

Many teachers work to extend the attention span of their students. While this is a noble pursuit, it is an uphill battle that does not need to be fought. Because television, radio, books, magazines, and nearly all other media are designed to work within the established attention span, a teacher's efforts would have little effect. It is better to simply file student attention spans under "accept the things I cannot change" and focus your energy on working with and within these limits.

Accepting short student attention spans does not mean that you cannot teach long lessons. It just means that you need to break them up somehow. Television and radio programs change topics and scenes frequently and break up their presentations with commercials about every five to seven minutes. Novels and movies run multiple story lines and change between them every few minutes as well. All you need to do as a teacher is take a lesson from the media all around you and your students, and create breaks to allow the students to refocus their attention every few minutes.

Forty-five Minutes

Forty-five minutes has an equally important significance in education. Efficiency experts have found, through research, that workers are more efficient if they take a five-minute break after every forty-five-minute period of concentrated work. In other words, the workers in the study who took a five-minute break every forty-five minutes (for a total of about fifty minutes of break time in an eight-hour day) actually got *more* work done than workers who did not take breaks (and, therefore, were "working" for almost an entire extra hour)!

The researchers found that workers' efficiency and quality of work began to drop after about forty-five minutes. The longer past this time workers were asked to concentrate and continue without a break, the more they did slower, poorer quality work. The problem was corrected with a short respite during which the workers were allowed to get up from their workstations, move around, and think about something else.

So what does this have to do with teaching? If full-grown adults cannot concentrate efficiently for more than forty-five minutes, neither can our students (or teachers!). They need to be given short breaks. They need to be allowed to stand up from their desks and stretch occasionally. They need to get off topic every once in a while so they can refocus after the break (and so do you!).

This, again, is a reason to design your lessons with winding pathways. More than that, it is a reason to rethink what you do with homework, tests, and block-schedule classes. If you assign homework that takes students more than forty-five minutes to complete, you should expect their work to be of lower quality at the end of the assignment. If you give a test that takes more than forty-five minutes to complete, you should expect students to have trouble toward the end. If you try to teach a class for eighty to ninety minutes, you should expect students to retain less and have more discipline problems at the end of class.

There is good news, though. This, unlike the five-minute attention span, is a battle that can be easily fought and won. You do not have to give shorter homework assignments (though your students would thank you if you did). You do not have to give shorter tests (see previous note). You do not even have to give up block scheduling. You simply need to teach your students about the problem and how to deal with it.

Teach your students to take a short break—get up and walk around—after forty-five minutes of work on homework. Allow them to get up and stretch during a test (as long as they don't wander around comparing their answers to everyone else's). Take five minutes in the middle of your block-schedule class to get off topic, stretch, talk about whatever is on their minds, and so forth. You can even use a timer to mark the middle of class and the end of the break.

You will find two benefits to this approach. The first is that your students will focus better during their work time (even before the break, because they know it is coming) and will do higher quality work. The second is that *you* will focus better during work time and do better quality teaching. You will be a more efficient worker.

20

THE (RAIL)ROADS OF CHANGE

This book has suggested changes in your thinking about and your approach to education—big changes. It seems appropriate, then, to discuss our natural resistance to change. We all resist change. Our current knowledge and practice is comfortable. Change takes us out of our comfort zone. This is not easy, especially for those of us who have been teaching for a long time. Each new thing we learn and try is a step out of our comfort zones.

It is called a comfort zone for a reason. Leaving it is *not* comfortable. But if we can *become* comfortable with something new, if we can *expand* our comfort zone, we can grow. Teachers ask students to do this all the time. Parents ask their children to do this all the time. Yet parents and teachers often find it difficult to do these same things themselves. There is a reason for this: change is easier when we are younger. Why? Simple. Youth is all about learning and changing. Young people can step out of their comfort zones more easily because their zones have not been totally established yet. The younger the student, the easier this is. The younger the student, the less a comfort zone has been established. *Everything* is new and different, so *nothing* is especially comfortable *or* uncomfortable. It is just status quo.

Adults, on the other hand, have stopped growing physically, have found and established their strengths and talents (and their weaknesses), and have established ways of going about their jobs and their daily lives. Most adults have not only *established* their comfort zone but also built thick stone walls around its periphery. For these people, trying new things can be *very* uncomfortable.

These are the people who, when approached with a new and different idea, will say, "I have always done it this way"; "I am comfortable with how I do things now"; or "There is nothing I can do to change my students."

Being fully grown and established in your ways, it is difficult to be fond of new ideas that require much change. But, since you have read this far, you probably understand that people, like plants, *must* constantly grow or we will wither and die. Growth for people is not just getting taller. It is also *learning*. Growth from learning is rarely *comfortable* and always *requires* change. How can we expect our students to be open to learning and trying new things when we are not?

Change for the sake of change alone is generally not a good idea, and not all changes are positive ones, but some changes, when made with a goal in mind, can be *very* positive. You will never know if a new idea will be positive or negative for *you* until you try it. "This is how it has always been" is a rotten excuse for avoiding change. "What has always been" is comfortable. It is safe. But the safety of what has always been does not allow room for improvement. No one has ever achieved greatness by doing only what had always been done before. Avoiding change simply because it is change can actually end up causing problems.

Take, for example, railroads. The standard gauge (distance between rails) for trains in the United States is four feet, eight and a half inches. When NASA engineers were designing the space shuttle, they had to make the solid rocket boosters (the rockets attached to the sides of the fuel tank when the shuttles took off) smaller in diameter than they would have liked. This was because the rockets had to be transported by train and had to fit through the pathways that existed for our four-foot-eight-and-a-half-inch railway system. Their new technology had to work with "what had always been."

American railroads all use that weird gauge: four feet, eight and a half inches—not even a round number. So why do we use such a strange number? Our railroads were built by English immigrants and that was how they were built in England. Why did England use this gauge? English railroads were built by the people who built the prerailroad tramways and that is the gauge *they* used. So why is that gauge used for trams? Trams were built by the same people who built wagons, using the same jigs and tools. Wagon wheels were spaced that far apart. Why were the wagons built this way? Wagons were built this way because of the wheel ruts that already existed in some of the long-distance roads in England. If the wagon wheels did not fit into these grooves, they were in danger of breaking their wheels. So where

THE (RAIL)ROADS OF CHANGE

Figure 20.1. By Cathy Klasek

did the wheel ruts come from? The initial ruts were made by Roman war chariots, which were all built to this same specification.

This means that our "modern" railway system and, in turn, NASA's space shuttle, was built around specifications for ancient Roman war chariots. So what horse's backside came up with four feet, eight and a half inches? Exactly. Roman chariots were built just wide enough to accommodate the backsides of two war horses.

The size and power of the world's foremost space vehicle was limited by two things: the size of a horse's back end, and "this is how we have always done it." The moral of the story? Change does not always equal improvement, but sticking to the status quo can cause problems too.

Consider the new ideas you have read and then try a few. Many of the ideas should prove useful and helpful. Some of the ideas may not work for you, but you won't know until you try. Keep the ideas that work for you. Let go of the rest.

21

GIGO

In the 1980s (at the beginning of the age of personal computers), the above acronym was widely used. It stands for "Garbage In, Garbage Out." The purpose of the term was to remind us that computers were simply machines that followed the instructions given to them. If the computer gave you an answer you did not like (garbage out), it was not the computer's fault. The problem was with the information or the instructions you put into the computer in the first place (garbage in).

The idea was to try to get people to be more careful with the information they entered into a computer so that they could receive more accurate and agreeable output. Some computer teachers even went so far as to explain that the reverse was also true and that GIGO could just as easily stand for "Good In, Good Out."

Both definitions of the acronym are completely correct, in regard to both computers and life in general. In fact, the philosophy behind the term can be expanded to apply to anything. Essentially, it is a way of saying that, in any endeavor, you get out what you put in. A half-hearted effort will produce lackluster results. The best results come only from the best efforts.

You will find this to be true of the application of the ideas in this book as well. If you want to get the maximum positive result from applying the principles of entertainment, sales, and marketing to your classroom, you are going to have to give each idea maximum thought and effort.

Figure 21.1. By Cathy Klasek

Good begets good. Garbage begets garbage: GIGO. Which definition will you use?

THE NEXT STEP

The scope of this volume is intentionally limited. It is an introduction only. The intent was to cover a great many ideas with an extreme economy of words, to explain a new point of view and spark your imagination as to potential classroom applications. There is, however, a downside to the economy of words. Concepts are introduced and summarized but not examined in detail. Just enough detail has been included to explain each idea and give an example or two where appropriate and necessary. The included information should be just enough for you to experiment with the ideas presented herein, apply them to your own teacher character's style, and form your own opinions as to their value in your classroom.

Should you choose to follow the ideas in the book to their logical conclusion, you will likely find further study on the topics of interest to you to be most helpful. Fortunately, there are a great many excellent books to be found on entertaining, sales, marketing, and more. Finding an authoritative work to increase your knowledge of the subjects of interest to you should be quite easy.

Whether you choose to extend your study of the concepts introduced here formally or through experimentation in your classroom, one thing is clear. If you are going to derive any benefit in improving your teaching and your students' achievement, you must not stop at the last sentence of the book.

The end of the book should be only the beginning of a long road of educational excellence—for you, your students, and the communities you serve.

A FINAL THOUGHT

The magicians you may see on television, on a stage, or at a party are merely creators of illusions. The real magicians of the world are educators. Only educators can create knowledge where ignorance once existed, responsibility from anarchy, order from chaos, lifelong learners from couch potatoes, and good citizens from class clowns. That is real magic—shaping the future by creating responsible, well-informed adults.

When the methods of entertainers, salespeople, and marketers are combined with the power of the educator—the *real* magician—the results can be *truly* amazing!

ABOUT THE AUTHOR

Christopher Bontjes is an educator with more than twenty years of classroom experience. He holds undergraduate and graduate degrees in music education from Western Illinois University. His position as a music educator has allowed him the opportunity to work with students ranging from kindergarten through college. He regularly works with groups that range in size from one or two students to more than one hundred at a time. His students have been recognized for excellence on local, state, and national levels. He is a member of the National Education Association and the National Association for Music Education.

Bontjes has been a magician all his life. The son of two magicians, he attended his first magicians' convention at the age of six months. He began performing in public at age 4. His lifelong pursuit of magic and entertainment has included study with the top thinkers, creators, and performers in magic. He has performed across the country for live audiences of one to seventeen thousand, ages three through over one hundred. He has performed for private parties, banquets, festivals, theaters, libraries, schools, trade shows, and magicians' conventions. He is a member of the Magic Circle of England, the International Brotherhood of Magicians, and the Society of American Magicians where he served as national president in 2012–2013.

Bontjes is available for speaking engagements and teacher workshops. For details, please contact him at info@nclbored.com.

www.ingramcontent.com/pod-product-compliance
Lightning Source LLC
Chambersburg PA
CBHW070334230426
43663CB00011B/2305